Educational Resource Management

Educational Resource Management

An international perspective

Derek Glover and Rosalind Levačić

First published in 2007 by the Institute of Education, University of London,
20 Bedford Way, London WC1H 0AL
www.ioe.ac.uk/publications

British Library Cataloguing in Publication Data:
A catalogue record for this publication is available from the British Library

ISBN 978 0 85473 781 9

Derek Glover and Rosalind Levačić assert the moral right to be identified as
the authors of this work.

Design by River Design (www.riverdesign.co.uk)
Page makeup by Hobbs the Printers
Printed by Elanders www.elanders.com

Contents

Foreword

Educational resource management is an area of educational leadership that suffers because many of those involved in the field lack understanding of the issues. Policy makers often fail to see the impact of the frameworks they have established for school and colleges. Teachers often feel trapped by systems that inhibit their true task of sharing the joy of learning. Parents and the wider community are often incapable of articulating what they want from education, and when this is known, they fail to exert the necessary pressure for appropriate levels of resourcing. That said, there is an increasing demand for explanations of the interaction between national and local educational resourcing for schools and colleges and the achievement (or otherwise) of educational objectives. This book is an attempt to explain the link between resourcing and its effect in the world of education.

The work stems from teaching undertaken by the authors for Masters and distance Masters courses at the Institute of Education, University of London. However, the content has been presented in such a way that it offers a view of educational resource management pertinent to all those who are involved in educational leadership and management, not simply university students. To this end it is an amalgam of both 'why we do it' and 'how we do it', rather than either a practical guide to educational resource management or a record of elements of macro- and micro-research.

Nevertheless the book contains examples of educational resource management in action drawn from both UK and international practice, commentary as shown in the research literature, and our own reflection on the rationale for effective educational resource management. Whilst predominantly concerned with school practice, there are similarities in further and higher education and so some of the supportive literature is drawn from these sources. We hope that we have been able to meet the needs of a diverse range of readers and users, both national and international, and that in sharing our findings we can enhance the educational experience of the coming generation – their education determines our future!

This book owes much to the research that students have kindly allowed us to share as examples of practice. We are grateful to them both for the material and for the reflection they have prompted.

1 Educational organisations and their environment

In this chapter we will:

- introduce a framework for analysing resource management in education and set this within an open systems model of inputs, processes and outputs/outcomes;

- distinguish between educational outputs and outcomes;

- outline some of the underlying considerations in decision-making to acquiring human and physical resources for schools and colleges;

- show how such management operates differently in centralised and decentralised educational systems;

- outline the budget management cycle as a framework for decision-making.

Educational resource management is a fascinating area of study because there is such a wide variety of practice, not only between developed and developing countries but also between countries that have similar living standards. The importance a country attaches to education is reflected in the proportion of the Gross Domestic Product (GDP) it spends on education. In 2005 the Organisation for Economic and Cultural Development (OECD) average was 5.6 per cent, varying between 8 per cent in Korea and 3.5 per cent in Turkey.[1] Countries also differ in the proportion of their education budget they allocate to the major sectors: pre-school, primary, secondary, tertiary and higher education. They differ too in the relative importance they place on public and private funding of education and in the roles that public and private sector institutions play in providing education. Further differences arise in the relative amounts that are allocated to the different types of educational resources, such as teachers, support staff, learning materials, equipment and buildings.

All of us are faced with limited resources, and this is particularly so for educational institutions, especially those in developing countries where public sources of funding are very limited and even poor parents are often required to pay school fees. It is therefore imperative that educational organisations manage their finances and resources efficiently in order to secure the maximum learning benefit for students. While teachers and parents generally have no doubts that extra spending, more resources and smaller classes produce better results, the academic research on this issue has not confirmed these beliefs unequivocally (Levačić and Vignoles 2002) and researchers disagree about the effects of resources on learning. Apart from problems of data and methods, one important reason for this disagreement is that the efficiency of educational organisations varies. So if resources are not managed efficiently, an increase in spending does not necessarily mean an increase in student learning.

A framework: input-output systems

Education is essentially a close relationship between the teacher and the students, and between the school or college and its local environment. This relationship is sometimes called an 'open system' because the educational organisation is subject to influences from the environment, or context, within which it functions. Within the external environment, the organisation functions as an input-output system in which internal processes link the inputs to the final production of outputs. There are three main elements in this input-output model:

- the external environment from which the school or college derives its raw material of students, acquires its other resources and to whom it supplies the outputs;

- the processes that take place within the organisation, known as the production technology;

- the human relations system that forms a bridge between the external environment and the organisation and which affects the way in which educational production is undertaken.

Because of the emphasis on the external environment (or context) and processes, this way of thinking about the educational organisation is referred to as the context-input-process-output model (Scheerens 1999).

The external environment within which organisations operate is influenced by a number of forces. Organisational theorists (for example, Butler 1991) often distinguish between the general environment and the task environment. The former is the combination of major technological, social, political and economic forces that influence educational policy. The latter, sometimes called the specific environment, is all the local influences that impact directly upon the school, including parents, the local community, and central and local government. Together these constitute the stakeholders of a school or college.

Butler (1991) argues that in order to survive, the organisation should pursue ends that broadly meet the needs of these stakeholders. This is because they exchange the inputs or resources – usually through fees, grants or local taxes – for the outputs that come from the activity. Applying Butler, within the general environment education has to compete with health, defence and other objectives to secure funding for resources. At the task environment level, there has to be a relationship with the local community to top up the resources and to offer actual and moral support. The ability of the local community to do this also depends upon a variety of factors, including the inhibiting or motivating effect of external regulation at both general and task levels.

Inputs or resources are obtained from the external environment and are used to support and create learning activities for students. Schools and colleges may receive both financial resources – that is, money – and real resources. For real resources, a distinction is made between human (i.e. all the people employed in a school or college) and physical resources (i.e. all those items necessary for the process of teaching and learning and pupil support). The most important of the real resources or inputs is staff: teachers, support staff and managers/leaders. Other key real inputs are buildings and infrastructure, equipment and learning materials, such as books. When a public sector school or college is allocated a budget by its funding authority, it is allocated financial resources which it uses to purchase real resources. In a very centralised system, schools and colleges receive all their resources in kind – that is, real resources are directly allocated. In decentralised finance systems, schools and colleges are allocated most or part of their resources in the form of finance. However, even in the most decentralised of school systems, such as England, state schools receive their buildings in kind and do not purchase them (apart from new capital works) or pay rent.

The model shown in Figure 1.1 below shows the educational process results in outputs and outcomes. These are the products of education systems. Outputs are the more immediate and measurable gains from education. At an individual level, outputs are examination achievement, sports team participation, degree results and many other personal gains. At an institutional level, these are the basis for league tables of results, and at the national level, aggregated data gives a picture of overall levels of mathematical, linguistic and scientific attainments which are used for comparison with chronological age, social deprivation or other criteria for longitudinal or international comparison.

Outcomes are the longer lasting and more general results of educational experience. At the individual level, they are seen in the balance of competence and confidence that enables participation in higher levels of employment, and social and community integration. At a national level, outcomes are reflected in levels of employment, crime rates, various forms of deprivation, psychological welfare and many more. These all contribute to public well-being and lead to the assertion that education is fundamental to national well-being.

The essential relationship is that between resources or inputs and the consequent learning achieved by students. In a survey of resource allocation in developing countries, Harber and Davies (1998) show that basic lack of resources, local ineptitude, low staff pay and corruption inhibit good-quality education. They report excessive pupil–teacher ratios (often over 100:1), lack of pens, pencils and basic textbooks, poorly paid and often underqualified staff, and inadequate buildings. This contrasts with national and international expectations of the role of education in securing economic and social improvement through Education For All.

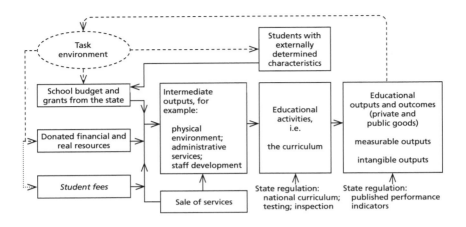

Figure 1.1   An educational organisation as an open system
(from: Levačić 2000: 11)

The conversion of resources into educational outputs and outcomes is depicted in Figure 1.1 as a progression from acquiring resources from the external environment, using these to support and create processes within the school in which teaching and learning takes place in order to produce educational outputs and outcomes for students. This is affected variously by the tension between central and local, or institutional, self-management. Local control over the use of resources is dependent upon the framework within which the school or college exists, the availability of resources to support activity and the nature of those competing for support. Accountability requires that state-funded schools should demonstrate that they are able to use resources efficiently and effectively, a recurring theme. Production technology cannot be applied efficiently unless schools and colleges know what they want to achieve, look at the ways in which they can do so, evaluate the methods available for the educational process and then move to implement plans. This goes alongside the management of resources through:

- the translation of the financial resources via the budget into real resources (i.e. human and material),
- the management of real resources so as to create and maintain the learning environment,
- the deployment of the resources acquired directly for learning to support teaching and learning.

(Levačić 1997: 132)

Resource and financial management

As already mentioned, in many systems, schools, and less often universities, are allocated real resources (i.e. buildings, teachers) in kind. Elsewhere educational organisations are allocated a global budget, expressed in money terms, from which they must purchase real resources. When a school or college has a delegated budget, a major responsibility of management is how to spend the budget to best effect to achieve the organisation's educational aims. There is an increasing tendency for educational organisations to be given a major degree of financial autonomy. It is argued that this will ensure that spending is related to local need and, in political terms, will hold the organisation accountable for the funds devolved for its use.

Accountability takes many forms. In essence it involves some way in which those to whom financial resources have been delegated have to explain how, why and to what effect these resources have been used. In general, the greater the autonomy in decision-making for resource management, the more the organisation, through its management and leadership, has to account for its stewardship. Those decisions affect both human and physical resources; we will return to them as we look at the detail of the budget process. Put at its simplest, resource management is about converting the inputs into outputs. What are the important considerations in doing this?

Staff selection, training and management

Human resources vary in quality. No two teachers bring exactly the same qualities to the classroom. Some are superb teachers but may be poor administrators; others may be less inspired teachers but have excellent class control and offer considerable pastoral support gifts. To some degree this variation is related to personality and innate abilities, but it can also be influenced by the person's initial education and subsequent training and experience. There has been a considerable move to enhance the consistency of human resource quality by using job and task analysis to identify the necessary competencies required in teaching or educational administration and leadership. Emphasis has also been placed on the development of training to meet identified competencies and the furthering of assessment to ensure that, as near as possible, two people of similar background and experience are equally capable of fulfilling their teaching role. Thus resource management involves leaders in schools and colleges ensuring that adequate continuing professional development takes place so that human resources are developed to meet changing needs. National policy can have important effects on human resources through, for example, state regulation of the quality of initial and in-service training available to teachers and other staff.

Determining the relative division between human and physical resources

In most developed countries the ratio of spending is approximately 80 per cent on human resources and 20 per cent on physical resources, although this is subject to enormous variation. Issues of class size, class ability grouping, support staff within the classroom and the school as an entirety, and the use of computer technology, textbooks and other materials of instruction, all require senior managers to estimate potential costs. The distinction between human and physical resources may not be as straightforward as it seems. A set of science textbooks is clearly a physical resource; so too is work by a maintenance contractor, but the development of a programme of self-supported learning draws upon both the physical resources (in the purchase of paper for the materials) and also human resources (emanating from the teacher who undertook the work of preparing the course). Senior managers then have to ascertain the contributions to enhanced outcomes if different combinations of human and physical resources are used.

Core and non-core activities

Core activities are those that have to be maintained if the school or college is to fulfil national or local requirements. These might include specific curriculum delivery, and learning objectives. Additionally though, educational organisations have varying degrees of freedom to offer non-core activities, including subject areas (for example, with music specialism), or opportunities to others who wish to use resources (for example, for adult or community education). Non-core activities may attract potential pupils or adult users (with the possibility of additional fee income), but the examination result outputs from core activities may be the 'league tables' by which the school is judged. Decision-making may require achieving a balance in fulfilling these differing objectives.

Current and capital expenditure

We shall return to look at this issue in depth, but at this point it is important to recognise that leaders may face making decisions relating to expenditure on capital resources, generally buildings and major items of equipment, and current resources used for the immediate work of classroom teaching. Where schools are poorly funded, there is a tendency for decision-making to be based on the need to have teachers in front of students and, as a result, there may be inadequate funds for the purchase of materials of instruction. Decisions aimed at reducing staff numbers to ensure properly equipping a science laboratory, for example, may be influenced by union power and parental reaction.

Centralised and decentralised financial allocation systems

To a great extent decision-making is also affected by the way in which the allocation of funds to the school or college is controlled. In broad terms we can differentiate between centralised and decentralised systems. Here we are concerned mainly with the distribution of decision-making power over resources to different levels, but we should bear in mind that the degree of centralisation or decentralisation can vary considerably in other domains of decision-making, such as curriculum, school evaluation, admissions, and regulating qualifications for education staff. In centralised systems all decisions with regard to the domain in question are made by a central authority and applied to all institutions, with limited opportunity for decision-making at the local level. In such systems, accountability for the outcomes from the allocation and use of resources remains with the central authority. In decentralised systems, there are varying degrees of autonomy in decision-making at the local level. Generally the finance is allocated to operational level and then resource decisions are taken within the school or college, subject to varying levels of guidance. However, decentralised systems reflect varying degrees of autonomy according to the powers and resource opportunities that have been delegated.

Three forms of decentralisation are defined:

- Deconcentration. This occurs when the central authority creates its own regional or local administrative units, or a specialised functional unit, and delegates specific decisions to these units (Hanson 1998). For example, in France in the 1980s the Ministry of Education deconcentrated the administration of primary and secondary education to 28 regional offices headed by central government appointees (Daun 2004). Deconcentration brings decision-making closer to the clients of the service but does not involve local democratic participation in decisions. *Authority*, however, is usually retained at the centre.

- Delegation. This is the transfer of decision-making responsibility from a higher level to a lower level authority, for example, from central to local government or to schools, but the transfer of power is not permanent: it can be revoked by the higher authority and returned to it if it so wishes. Delegation increases local autonomy and permits greater efficiency in meeting local needs, but usually within central guidelines or constraints. Local units are usually made accountable to the centre as well as to local clients.

- Devolution. This permanently transfers decision-making power from a higher to a lower level authority and so allows considerable local accountability and local autonomy. Resources are allocated to the local level with freedom to develop strategies and policies within broad frameworks. As a result there are opportunities for enhanced allocative efficiency but the systems operating locally could well be inefficient and productive efficiency therefore lower.

This is a somewhat simplistic analysis, but it does highlight the need for balance between accountability and autonomy at central or local level and, within that, the optimisation of resource use according to local need. When schools and colleges work within a devolved or delegated system, this is often referred to as 'autonomy'. While this means that the school or college has allocated funds and freedom for resource decision-making, there are constraints, for example, in defining targets for outcomes or in allocating additional funding for specific use within tight frameworks. Caldwell's definition makes clear the balance of freedoms and constraints:

> A self-managing school is a school in a system of education to which there has been decentralised a significant amount of authority and responsibility to make decisions related to the allocation of resources within a centrally determined framework of goals, policies, standards and accountabilities.
>
> (Caldwell 2002: 35)

Decision-making for schools and colleges takes place within a system determined by the decentralisation of function (for example, employment of staff) and decentralisation of organisation level (for example, at local or district level, or at school or college level). Eurydice, an information network for the European Union, analysed the complexity of decentralisation of educational funding in Europe in 2001 and showed the great variation in decentralisation, both of function and organisation. Systems are complex: for example, in French-speaking Belgium all funding and decision-making regarding teaching, staff resources, buildings and equipment are taken at governmental level only, but decisions regarding teaching equipment is funded by the municipality, with further decision-making within the funds devolved to school level. Table 1.1 illustrates this complexity for two other countries.

Table 1.1 **Comparison of funding and decision-making for education in Austria and Portugal**

Element	Austria		Portugal	
	Funded by	**Decisions by**	**Funded by**	**Decisions by**
Teaching staff	Central govt.	Regional govt.	Central govt.	School council
Non-teaching staff	Municipality	Municipality	Central govt.	School council
Maintenance	Central and regional govt.	Headteacher	Central govt.	School council
New building	Central and regional govt.	Central and regional govt.	Central and regional govt.	Central and regional govt.
Books and materials	Municipality	Headteacher	Central govt.	School council
School meals	Municipality	Municipality	Central govt. and municipality	School council
Transport	Central social fund	Central social fund	Central govt.	Central govt.

In some centralised systems, allocating staff and providing teaching and learning resources is organised entirely by central or regional government. In some systems, teachers are allocated to schools by a central staffing office; in others, only the responsibility for funding staffing is centrally held, and appointments are made at regional or school level, while in yet other systems, the central authority allocates a basic number of staff but then allows the school to purchase and appoint additional staff from its delegated resources. Similarly it is common for schools in decentralised systems to be required to provide a certain basic staffing, or to follow curriculum guidelines. Thus, although these are examples of an apparently delegated responsibility, they have statutory force and cannot be ignored. Such a system ensures that schools with delegated resource functions act within national or local guidelines.

Resources for new buildings are frequently allocated by central government, but plans are regionally implemented. School transport is also frequently centrally funded but regionally planned. In short, the two elements of resourcing schools and colleges – funding and implementation – have been part of a complex system. There are increasing pressures for implementation to be devolved to the lowest possible level so that accountability is rendered to the community being served.

An organisation can be placed on a continuum between total centralisation and total decentralisation for all its resources. The differences are seen in the decentralisation of provision and control of the following items:

- buildings;

- buildings maintenance;

- teaching staff;

- administrative staff;

- non-teaching support staff;

- administrative services, for example, telephone, computer technology;

- non-teaching equipment;

- teaching equipment;

- books;

- stationery.

There is also a great variation in the number of levels of control. Some countries settle policy at national level and then delegate issues of resource allocation to districts; some delegate all educational matters to district authorities, while others delegate educational organisation to the local district. Within the local district there are then varying requirements for resource allocation to be further delegated to the school. The systems are complex and the implications for resource management considerable because it is not simply a matter of allowing schools the freedom to act independently, but also requiring that they function within the strictures of a given accountability framework. This framework may control the entire educational enterprise including governance, vision and objective setting, curriculum organisation and control, quality assurance systems and staff development.

Resource allocation is the mediating process through which all these function. At an institutional level it may affect the levels of staffing, the replacement of poorer buildings, the acquisition of teaching equipment and many other factors. The impact is felt not only by individual pupils, but also by the school, the community at large, and ultimately impacts upon the national picture. The way in which resources are used may be more effective in some schools or higher education departments than in others, especially if published tables of achievements in public examinations are used as a guide to schools' effectiveness. The effect of this is that some institutions may appear to be more attractive to potential students or, more likely, their parents, and as a result they may grow. If national resourcing is devolved on a per capita basis then successful schools attract more funds and can appear to be favoured. Meanwhile, schools that are declining will lose funds – this may be a spur to improvement or the signal for yet further decline.

In a study of the decentralisation of education in Japan, Hiromitsu Muta (2000) points to other national contextual factors that affect resource allocation. In the 1980s there were pressures in Japan, with its highly centralised and hierarchical organisation of education, to move from a closed, overly standardised and inward-looking system towards one that would encourage personnel development and creativity. The need for change was exacerbated by the declining urban birth rate, which offered opportunities for institutional competition. Regulations were relaxed to abolish the appointment-approval system, formerly exercised by prefecture superintendents, to establish greater school autonomy, to establish local standards for class size, and to distinguish between instructions and orders, and guidance and advice. Local autonomy has increased and curricular and organisational freedom has been more fully exploited according to local need. However, as deregulation has progressed, educational gaps between schools and areas have widened, the pupil roll – and hence income – of the less successful schools has fallen, staffing ratios have worsened and the intended creativity has been stifled because of the need to conform to national government attainment targets. Resource allocation is now being more tightly controlled at national and local level in an attempt to support those schools that are apparently less successful because of the nature of their socio-economic context. It is hoped that supplementary funding will enable all schools to be effective by compensating for the effects of underfunding where pupil numbers are declining.

The budgetary cycle

Most financial and resource management is determined through the operation of the budgetary cycle. This offers a framework for the various processes that lead to the systematic management of resources.

There are four main phases in the budget management cycle:

- generating the budget by obtaining resources;

- allocating (planning) the budget for the following year (or several years);

- implementing the budget plan through financial control procedures;

- evaluating the use of the budget so as to improve decision-making in the future.

Budget generation

The initial, generation, stage is for the organisation to recognise just what financial support it will have in the coming period (usually one year). It is essential for most organisations to obtain resources from the external environment. As we shall see in the next chapter, generating income can be problematic, especially where national or district instability leads to fluctuations in the public funds that are available for use in any one year. Funds may be generated from a variety of sources and not simply allocated from public funds; indeed, for the private sector all funds have to be generated from other sources. This means that these institutions cannot set fee levels until potential income has been realistically considered.

Allocation

At the same time as financial managers have to be aware of potential income, they also need to have a system for considering and allocating resources for the purchase of the various human and physical resources that are needed to fulfil the educational programmes that were agreed in the allocation phase. In general, the organisation will be aware of what it needs to spend to meet the objectives and have alternative plans to secure the same objectives, but there may be differing views of the balance of resources to achieve the planned outputs and outcomes. We will consider allocation in greater detail in Chapters 5 and 6.

Implementation

Having established how potential resources and planned expenditure can be brought into balance, those responsible for budgets then have to implement the programme and ensure that the resources are used according to the plans. In this implementation phase, financial control procedures have to be in place to ensure that purchases accord to good practice and that there is no misuse of funds. This is not to say that any deviation from the original plan is not acceptable, merely that it should be in accordance with agreed financial procedures, and properly recorded and controlled. Adjusting planned expenditure is sensible when unexpected changes occur in the course of the year, but such changes must have soundly based reasons and not prevent the budget from breaking even.

Evaluation

The final stage of the budget cycle occurs after the completion of the accounting period. During this evaluation phase those responsible consider the extent to which they have, or have not, secured their objectives in the budget and explain any deviations from the intended plan. Evaluation includes assessing the quality of previous budget decisions and checking what effect they had. This is the accountability phase of the budget when findings and observations from the public authority or private board responsible for the school, college or department then form a basis for future planning and the cycle begins again.

While these four phases follow the above sequence for the budget of a financial year, at any one time a school or college can be engaged in all four stages – maintaining support in the external environment and ensuring future revenues, planning next year's budget, implementing and monitoring the current year's budget and, possibly, evaluating spending decisions from the previous year's budget.

Conclusion

In this chapter we have set out the background to the conversion of funds (the inputs) through a variety of educational practices (the processes) to outputs and outcomes. Underpinning this open systems model is the need for decision-making so that scarce resources are used to secure the aims and objectives of the public or private bodies responsible for education provision at whatever level. This decision-making process is given form and structure through the budget cycle, but we also need to consider further a set of terms that enable consistent assessment and understanding of the way in which resources are used.

---

[1] The OECD's annual publication *Education at a Glance* gives these and many other statistics on education.

2 Funding education – public and private systems

In this chapter we will:

- introduce the key principles used in evaluating the allocation and use of resources: adequacy, effectiveness, efficiency, value for money, transparency and equity;

- consider the efficiency and equity arguments for public and private funding, and the public and private provision of education;

- distinguish between the private and public benefits of education;

- outline the sources of funding for education and the institutions engaged in the provision of education: the public–private split.

A fundamental principle of funding is that resources are scarce; therefore there is always a finite amount of funding for education. This consideration should underpin all decision-making. If finance was not limited, the constraints within which education processes evolve would be very different, leading to the employment of as many teachers as necessary for maximising learning, as many textbooks and as much science equipment and technology as teachers felt were required and as much support as was thought to produce the best outcomes. But the reality is that resources are limited: as desirable as any educational objective might be, it can only be secured if funding is available. This is not only the case from central or local sources, but also from public and private sources. Judging the potential best use of these resources requires an understanding of certain economic terms.

Key principles

It is necessary to have some criteria by which the use of resources can be judged. These are concerned with the way in which resource use affects outputs and outcomes.

Adequacy

Adequacy means that the level of resourcing is sufficient to meet defined educational standards or objectives at national, district and local levels. The concept of adequacy has been well tested in US courts since US education policy is made through cases that challenge whether particular practices are constitutional. Many cases have been mounted on the basis that particular states' funding of education for particular districts or students was not adequate. Working out an adequate level of resourcing is not straightforward and there are a number of approaches. A simple method, and one now abandoned in US courts, is to compare education expenditure per student with an average, for example, the average over state school districts. As Odden and Picus (1992: 72) note, US courts have changed the assessment of adequacy in terms of the resources needed to enable educational programmes that provide for a minimum high standard of education for most students. This involves defining learning objectives, setting a curriculum and testing standards reached and then costing the resources for providing the curriculum. This approach can be further refined by estimating the resource levels that are required by students with different learning needs. This approach to adequacy means assessing the amount of compensatory finance that is needed to bring disadvantaged students up to defined minimum standards.

Policy makers have tried to define adequate spending level in three major ways:

- identifying a set of required inputs and pricing them;

- linking spending per pupil to a level of student outcomes, by identifying districts that produce the desired outcomes, selecting average-performing students, then calculating average spending per pupil;

- building a total amount from the bottom up by identifying the cost of each school-wide programme that produces desired outcomes.

The adequacy of the level of national spending on education can be judged roughly by making international comparisons. Data from *Education at a Glance*, the annual digest of statistics provided by the Organisation for Economic and Cultural Development (OECD), show an enormous variation in education expenditure per student. In 2004 Switzerland and the USA spent an average of $12,000 per student per year, much of Europe spent near to the OECD median of $7,500 per student per year and, at the lower end of the expenditure range, the Russian Federation, Brazil and Turkey spent less than $1,500 per student per year. In part these differences reflect differences in GDP per capita: poorer countries spend less per student on teacher salaries because salaries are generally lower for all occupations; nevertheless an equivalent number of teachers are being mobilised for a much lower cost than in developed countries. Differences are also due to the greater numbers of students in the high-spending countries in tertiary (university) education, which is more expensive than general education. We must stress that:

> Lower unit expenditure does not necessarily lead to lower achievement and it would be misleading to equate lower unit expenditure generally with lower quality of educational services. For example, the cumulative expenditure per student between primary and secondary education of Korea and the Netherlands are below the OECD average and yet both were among the best-performing countries in the PISA 2003 survey.
>
> (OECD 2006: 171)

A more meaningful statistic for comparing the resources countries allocate to education is to compare education spending as a percentage of GDP. The proportion of national resources devoted to education is determined in part by national policy, and in part by the priority given to education relative to other areas of the public and private sectors:

> The amount of national resources devoted to education depends on a number of interrelated factors of supply and demand, such as the demographic structure of the population, enrolment rates, income per capita, national levels of teachers' salaries, and the organisation and delivery of instruction. The size of the school-age population in a particular country shapes the potential demand for initial education and training. The larger the number of young people, the greater the potential demand for educational services. Among OECD countries of comparable national income, a country with a relatively large youth population will have to spend a higher percentage of its GDP on education so that each young person in that country has the opportunity to receive the same quantity of education as young people in other OECD countries. Conversely, if the youth population is relatively small, the same country will be required to spend less of its wealth on education in order to achieve similar results.
>
> (OECD 2006: 203)

This explains why, although Denmark and New Zealand spend a comparable 7 per cent of their GDP on education, the provision yields more educational resources per student in Denmark where there is a lower proportion of 5–29-year-olds passing through the educational system. Differences in the age profile of populations are removed if we compare education spending per student as a percentage of GDP per capita. The OECD average for primary education in 2003 was 20 per cent, ranging from 28 per cent in Italy to 13 per cent in Turkey and the Czech Republic (OECD 2006).

But it is not only national policy that determines resourcing for education. There can be variations at local level, for example, where the national per capita allocation or a devolved global sum is supplemented to meet local socio-economic conditions either from national or local funding. This is markedly so in the USA where local taxation related to property values puts some areas at a great advantage. It is also a feature of East African countries where there is a heavy dependence on local funding and so a variation in standards between urban and rural areas.

In poor countries that place an emphasis on basic literacy and numeracy, that have low wage levels for teaching staff and minimal building provision, the amount of money deemed adequate to fund a school of 100 pupils will be very low by contrast with the apparent needs of countries where the concept of basic education extends to secondary or even to higher education. The answer to the adequacy conundrum is political, and governments need to be persuaded of the benefits accruing from education to make more public resources available.

Effectiveness

This refers to the extent to which an organisation is judged to meet its objectives, regardless of cost. Effectiveness is a concept used for non-profit organisations which, by definition, cannot be judged on profitability. It is a concept that endeavours to bring together both the measurable and the more subjective elements of education hinted at in the previous section. It is the relationship between a school's objectives and its outputs, but both of these are difficult to quantify – and yet a 'hunch' about whether a school is effective or not in relation to its objectives may be an important reflection of the way in which it is using its resources. It is a concept that embraces an implicit (if not always explicit) assumption that the objectives set for public sector schools reflect the social value of the outputs and outcomes produced by schools. A standard definition of effectiveness evolved by the UK Audit Commission is: 'how well a programme or activity is achieving its established goals or other intended effects' (1984: 3). With this in mind, a school or college is effective if it meets its objectives fully, but is 'high cost' if it uses its resources wastefully. This could be the case for effective schools with small classes.

Efficiency

Efficiency is the relationship between an institution's inputs and its outputs. Efficiency entails securing minimum inputs for a given quality and quantity of education provided. This is achieved when a given quantity of output is produced at minimum cost. Defining and measuring the outputs of schools and colleges is problematic. For one, schools are multi-product enterprises – students learn a great variety of social skills and attitudes as well as specific cognitive knowledge and skills. Cognitive attainment, as measured in tests, exams and qualifications, is the most frequently used measure of output, but it only captures a part of a school's output.

As noted in Chapter 1, the term 'output' is usually restricted to the immediate measurable effects of school or university, for example, in terms of exam results. 'Outcomes' of schooling are longer term and include employability, earning capacity and non-monetary benefits of education such as better health, better informed decision-making and enjoyment of cultural activities.

Efficiency as the relationship between inputs and outputs (or outcomes) can be illustrated by a simple example. Two schools have 70 per cent of their leavers achieving a certain level of basic literacy, but School A spends less per pupil than School B. Provided that the students in the two schools have the same distribution of prior attainment scores when entering the school, then we can conclude that A is more efficient.

This concept is further refined by distinguishing between *technical efficiency*, which is the relationship between physical units of the inputs and the outputs (i.e. classrooms, teaching ratios, textbooks and so on), and *productive efficiency*, which is the minimum cost method of production. *Technical efficiency* is the relationship between the combinations of different inputs used and the resulting quantity of output. This can be seen in education where the inputs of teaching and materials of instruction are used in different combinations to produce a given number of pupils attaining a specified examination level. Several methods are assumed to be available – some more teacher-intensive, others making greater use of texts and technology. For each method, it can be assumed that the different combinations of teacher hours and equipment produce the same output. If it is not possible to produce the same amount of output with less of one input without increasing the amount of another input, then that combination of inputs is technically efficient. There can be lots of technically efficient combinations of inputs.

However, *productive efficiency* requires using the cheapest combination of inputs, which depends on the relative prices of the inputs. The technically efficient combination of teachers and equipment, given prevailing input prices, that produces an output most cheaply is known as the cost-efficient (or price-efficient) combination. Thus if teachers become more expensive compared to computers, then it is cost-efficient to use more computers and fewer teachers, provided that output (i.e. student learning) does not decline.

Educational productivity is related to the concept of efficiency, but relates the amounts of inputs used to achieve the outputs. Given the amount of other resources teachers work with, then the greater the output per teacher, the lower the cost per unit of output (given constant salaries) – in short, the bigger the class, the lower the unit cost. Technical progress is important in the economy generally as it is the main means of raising productivity. Better methods of teaching can raise teacher productivity. New technologies (computer-assisted learning and e-learning) are proffered as potential ways of raising productivity in education, but have yet to prove themselves. Miller and Glover (2006) have shown that, while it is possible to evaluate new technology in the classroom qualitatively, it is difficult to identify and measure the contribution that it actually makes to learning.

Productivity is a complex issue in education. For instance, some teachers are regarded as more productive than others, although this is difficult to measure reliably. The quality of teacher A may differ from teacher B and yet their cost per hour is the same; a set of texts used by teacher C may be less efficient than when they are used by teacher D, and so on. Pupil and student inputs may be comparable where basic intelligence or reading age is measured, but there can be little measurement of personality factors, attitude and behavioural traits. Levačić comments that:

> The problem facing teachers and school managers in making resource decisions, especially those concerning the most efficient and productive mix of learning resources and educational activities, is the absence of a well specified technical knowledge base which gives a blueprint of efficient methods.
>
> (Levačić 1997: 135)

The definition of efficiency used so far has been the *internal efficiency* of educational organisations. Internal efficiency takes the social value of output as given (for example, basic literacy) and is only concerned with minimising the cost of this output. *External efficiency* refers to the value society places on the outputs produced by productive units, such as firms, schools, hospitals, etc. By contrast, internal efficiency is limited to producing a given output at minimum cost.

The issue of whether the outputs of schools or universities are of value to society is a separate one. Colleges could be very efficient at producing pastry cooks, for example, when society does not value these skills because nobody wants to eat cakes. Firms operating in competitive markets in the private sector have a direct signal of whether society values what they produce – their level of profits. Public sector institutions do not have such signals and so need criteria other than profitability to judge the value of their outputs. An important method of valuing output not produced for sale on markets is the political process – people vote for public policies and expenditure on public sector funded goods and services. There are also economic techniques for valuing non-market output, such as cost-benefit analysis.

Value for money

If an activity or an organisation is both efficient and effective, it is said to be providing value for money. This concept attempts to bring the measurable and the immeasurable, the objective and the subjective together. Glyn attempts to define value for money as 'a situation where those who strive to provide the service do the best they can with the resources that are available' (1987: 12). Interpretations of 'best they can' will vary according to the views of the observers. Value for money is used in two ways. One has already been defined:

the outputs compared to the inputs judged in terms of effectiveness and efficiency. The second definition is more limited, being restricted to the requirement that the resource managers attain the best-value purchases (for example, by having several competitive price quotations) and that they subsequently evaluate what they have purchased against the needs of the organisation.

Kremer *et al.* (1997) looked at these issues in the development of education in Kenya. In their work, the authors were concerned to establish the practicalities of changing the balance of teachers and other elements in education. They analysed both resource provision and resource use. They concluded that while schools had been encouraged to recruit to, and beyond, physical capacity, and while greater rolls mean a greater income entitlement, there was no positive link to quality because of the great variation in the quality of headship, financial and resource management, and the community's capacity to raise additional funds. In their view, external assistance is best offered to parents in a poor area rather than to the school itself, as then parents, as consumers, can determine where the money is spent. This, they argue, helps good schools to grow rather than simply putting additional funds into schools in poor areas, which are likely to be of poor or indifferent quality.

Over the last 20 years, it has been argued that both internal and external efficiency and value for money in the public sector has improved as a result of the introduction of some element of market forces. There has been an increasing and worldwide movement towards some degree of self-government for schools in the past 30 years. Within nationally prescribed frameworks and the retention of some central control through setting and monitoring standards, individual schools or colleges have been allowed to function without detailed central control, particularly over inputs. This has led to the development of quasi-markets, for example, by allowing parents freedom of choice in selecting schools. This has increased the degree of competition between schools in attracting students and is accompanied by funding schools largely in terms of the number of pupils they enrol.

Transparency

We have already stressed that education is affected by political pressures. There is a need for all those involved in making the decisions that determine funding to be given the necessary information to enable them to make sound judgements that can be shown to be so. This requires the system to be transparent, which depends on how much information is available in the public domain. When decisions are made at the local level and within schools and colleges, the public needs to know how devolved funds have been allocated, whether they have been properly spent and to what extent the resources have met the objectives set by or for schools. The need for transparency is recognised in various ways, with national allocation and reporting systems being available in the public domain. This has the combined effect of encouraging democratic involvement and lessening the opportunities for corrupt practice and siphoning off of funds. Transparency is a necessary feature of accountability. Without it, the framework and the impact of reporting to funding authorities, be it at local or national levels, will be inhibited.

Equity

One of the foremost concerns of the public in any area is that they are being treated fairly by their local area, their national government and the world at large. An example of differences in resourcing is the enormous variation in resources to support information and communications technology (ICT) learning. The percentage of headteachers reporting a serious lack of ICT equipment ranged from 2 per cent in Iceland, to 5 per cent in Finland and 27 per cent in Greece, and 45 per cent in Turkey (OECD 2006).

These figures reflect the varying ability of countries to generate national income as well as differing policy decisions on what percentage of national finance should be available to schools. While such differences across national boundaries can be understood, there is much greater parent and student unhappiness about variations in the level of funding to schools and colleges in different areas within a country. This leads us to think further about equity in the allocation of resources to different institutions and other units, and then to students, subjects or other curricular programmes. What distribution is judged fair is a highly subjective matter. Most equity judgements involve a great deal of thought about the social ends of education as interpreted within the context of a school or college. Equity is a complex concept and has several distinct interpretations. One distinction is between equality of opportunity (people are able to make the same choices) and equality (people have the same amount of an item, such as income or education).

Another important distinction is between horizontal and vertical equity. Applied to education, horizontal equity is the criterion that students with similar needs should receive the same amount of resources. Vertical equity is the criterion that students with greater learning needs should receive more resources – though how much more is a difficult issue to resolve. 'Fairness' judgements can be based on comparisons of unit costs – how much is the school spending per pupil on teaching mathematics to pupils at different levels, for example – but most equity judgements do involve a great deal of thought about the social ends of education as interpreted within the context of a school or college. For example, should examination-level classes be smaller than those where basic education is being taught; should pupils in a socially advantaged area have the same level of state support as those who are less favoured, and should schools be allowed to maintain small classes for university entrance qualifications when these lead to an uneconomic use of teaching resources and are thus a drain on local funding?

Important equity issues arise when some areas in a country are wealthier and can raise more tax to fund education than poorer areas. By contrast, poorer areas often have greater need for funding of education because of lack of parental support. This problem is tackled by a redistribution of tax revenues from richer and less needy areas to the poorer and more needy. This is known as fiscal equalisation. Benson and Marks (2005) see this as 'Robin Hood' funding, but note that even where redistribution does occur, the favoured areas often face overall lower costs than those needing assistance. An example of this would be where the socio-economic climate of the favoured areas results in lower crime rates and consequent lower building security costs. Some attempt at financial equalisation is practised in almost all European countries, often by supplements to the basic per capita formula for financial allocation. However, in many developing countries, such as China, central government does not have sufficient tax-raising powers to undertake this and so they have introduced other support measures. In China basic education is funded at provincial, county and community level (and so is very much affected by local income levels) but may also be supported by the income generated from local school-based enterprises. With such complex funding, it is difficult to promote equity. However, with rising prosperity and improved tax collection, a country like China can improve the situation.

The extent of centralising resource allocation can also affect equity issues. Where central allocation systems operate, it is easier to use funding mechanisms aimed at overcoming deprivation, for example, through allocating additional funding to socially deprived areas, or providing particular enhancement programmes aimed at meeting national objectives. If the allocation is decentralised, the authority to which allocation has been delegated could have other priorities and, if the overall delegated scheme is not prescriptive, it could, for example, maintain a per capita funding that does not address social needs. The development of quasi-markets may encourage schools to recruit more able students and avoid recruiting those from socially deprived backgrounds, thereby inhibiting equity (as outlined in recent developments in Japan in Chapter 1).

The private and public benefits of education

'Individuals and countries that invest in education and skills benefit economically and socially from that choice' (OECD 2006: 15). Human capital is a major factor driving economic growth, both in the world's most advanced economies and in those experiencing rapid development. Not least, it contributes tangibly to social outcomes, including health and social cohesion. It is noteworthy that rising tertiary education levels among citizens seem generally not to have led to an 'inflation' of the labour-market value of qualifications: among the countries with the largest expansion of tertiary education, in which the proportion of 25 to 64-year-olds with tertiary qualifications has increased by more than five percentage points since 1995 – Australia, Austria, Belgium, Canada, Denmark, Finland, Iceland, Ireland, Japan, Korea, Mexico, Poland, Spain, Sweden, Switzerland and the USA – most have seen stable or rising earnings benefits among tertiary graduates. This suggests that 'an increase in knowledge workers does not necessarily lead to a decrease in their pay in the way it does for low-skilled workers' (OECD 2006: 23).

Educational outputs and outcomes thus affect private and public well-being. Some would argue that education has value for its own sake and that the acquisition of knowledge and the development of skills and attitudes is important for the gain it can bring to individual development. While this is certainly true, it is the collective demand for education that determines public willingness to accede to national taxation systems to support education. It is public outputs and public outcomes that are used to justify the redirection of a proportion of the gross domestic product towards education. However, while the concepts can be understood, their measurement is difficult, as shown in the analysis of the returns to education in Honduras below. By this we mean the gains in income for individuals and in aggregate for the country as a result of the investment in schools and colleges.

Bedi and Edwards (2002) attempted to see how the quality of schooling contributed to earnings as a measure of educational outcomes in a study in Honduras. Their analysis demonstrates the difficulty of measurement in educational assessment because not all gains can be quantified, for example, espousal of democratic processes. Their aims were to see how far the quality of education resulted in higher earnings and, if this was the case, to investigate the role of education in securing a better distribution of earnings and, hence, opportunity. By identifying a number of factors that might affect educational outcomes, such as family background, teacher training profiles and school characteristics (availability of water and electricity), and then using regression analysis (a statistical process that establishes the effect of one factor on all the others), they were able to substantiate their hypothesis that educational quality and future earning are related.

For them, as for countless other commentators, education does make a difference. The outcomes and outputs are significant at a personal, local and national level. However, it is important to recognise that such exercises are generalisations – the authors point out that they were measuring the earnings of people in the current educational context, although the better method would have been to compare earnings now with the quality of education at the time when the cohort was at school! They also admitted that they were taking data of average earnings within a municipality as the basis of comparison when it would have been more accurate to relate earnings to the actual schools that individuals had attended. That said, their work is an example of how data on educational outcomes can be related to schooling.

In the eighteenth century Adam Smith recognised that education is an investment in human capital analogous to that of physical capital in the world of industry. Educational literature refers to economic capital as the present value of a flow of anticipated income. Present value means the value today of money received at specified future dates. The further away a given future sum of money is, the lower its present value. Present values also depend on interest rates, since the alternative to receiving £100 in the future – say in 10 years' time – is to receive a lower sum of money today which, when invested at the current rate of interest, equals £100 in 10 years' time. Clearly the higher the interest rate, the lower the present value of £100. Cultural capital and social capital are different from human capital. Cultural capital, like human capital, is the property of individuals and exists as long-lasting dispositions of the mind related to having the knowledge and skills to succeed in social relations. Social capital is the property of groups and is the aggregate of potential benefits arising from group membership. The interrelationship between these three is varied and complex but the notion of 'conversion' by which an activity in one area, for example, culture, affects outcomes in another, for example, economics, is fundamental to our understanding of the values and process of education. This understanding is affected by considering the ways in which education can be seen as a private (i.e. personal), or a public (i.e. collective) good.

At one level the outcomes of education are the personal gains. Student willingness to embark on higher education is determined in part by the personal advantages that are likely to accrue from participation. In reporting on research into graduate employability in a technical university in England, Glover and Law (2002) note that 58 per cent of students were attracted to higher education because of its anticipated effects on their earning capacity. The private rate of return to education is considered as the average percentage increase in earnings gained by a student moving from one level of education to the next higher level. Variations are shown: for the UK this was an average of 18 per cent increase in 2004 compared with levels in 2000, for Hungary 17 per cent, for Belgium 12 per cent, and for Sweden and Denmark 8 per cent (OECD 2006).

While these variations may be the result of differing labour market conditions, they still constitute a private inducement to proceed to higher levels of education. There are gains at all educational levels. These include the direct gains through basic literacy, numeracy and other knowledge visible from pre-school to higher education and measurable by test results and academic achievement. Personal gains include those wider skills that enable the individual to function in society. These also include the so-called 'key skills' of teamwork, problem-solving, communication and, increasingly, the use of technology. At a higher level the gains are in social interaction, moral development and creative capacity. At a local level these contribute to the availability of a skilled, or at least trainable potential workforce; at a national level they ensure that the needs of national policy development can be met. Education not only increases the private earnings of individuals, it also increases national output over and above its effects on individuals' earnings. This is because a more highly educated and skilled labour force adapts to technical change more quickly, thus raising the speed at which innovations are diffused through the economy and thereby raising productivity and growth of GDP.

While investment in education may occur, it does not automatically raise earnings and national economic growth rates. This will not arise if the quality of education is poor or if there is insufficient growth in the capital stock to absorb the additional more highly educated individuals or if they have studied areas that do not equip them for available jobs. In some countries graduate unemployment is a problem. Other contextual factors can inhibit the beneficial effects of education. For example, Ntshoe (2003) detailed this with evidence drawn from South Africa where ineffective governance and management and the ever-present problem of HIV/AIDS inhibits both outputs at an individual level and outcomes in general terms.

The educational economist, Eric Hanushek, has investigated the link between the development of human capital, and personal and national income growth. In a recent article, he presents evidence to show that it is not the number of years of schooling (or quantity of education) but the nature of teaching and learning (or quality of education) that has the greatest effect on employment and earnings potential. This investigation involved relating estimates of countries' cognitive attainment (based on international comparative tests since the mid-1960s with economic growth). He argues that, 'there is mounting evidence that quality measured by test scores is directly related to individual earnings, productivity, and economic growth' (Hanushek 2006: 449). He contends that the quality of work-related training schemes must be very high if they are to offer equivalent cognitive development to good-quality schooling, and that all reform requires enhanced teaching quality. These issues of curriculum content, process and teaching ability are fundamental to optimum resource use.

Funding education – public and private systems

The central issue for educational finance is what should be the respective roles of the public and private sectors in education. The relative importance of the two sectors varies between countries for political and historical reasons.

There are two main reasons for the state needing to contribute to financing education. The first is equity so as to ensure that children's educational opportunities are not determined by the income and preferences of their parents or guardians. The other is for reasons of efficiency, which arise from the fact that education has external benefits for society as a whole, as well as private benefits to the individual. Examples of the external benefits of education are a more productive workforce that enhances the rate of economic growth, social cohesion, better health and parenting, and better informed public decision-making through democratic political processes. If the external benefits of education are available to everyone regardless of whether they pay for them, there is no incentive for private individuals to finance public benefits. If this is so, the private education 'market' will not produce as much of the good in question as society (or part of that society) would wish to have available. Therefore a collective decision must be made to raise taxes and purchase the good through the state.

However, the state can ensure that more education is produced by financing it, for example, by paying for children to go to school: it does not need to enter production and be a provider as well. The distinction between the state financing education and actually providing it (i.e. producing it) is an important one. An important and controversial issue is whether state educational organisations are as internally efficient as private sector ones. It is argued that production units (for example, schools) are less efficient in the public sector than in the private sector because the former are protected from competition. Because of this, managers, teachers and lecturers have no incentives to work efficiently because they have secure public sector jobs and their salaries are paid regardless of performance. These arguments have underpinned recent educational policies in many countries. These include 'privatisation' or a greater reliance on private sector profit- and non-profit- making organisations that provide supplements to basic education that is still funded by the state.

In many developing countries the state cannot raise sufficient tax revenues to provide universal free basic education. A further problem in state schools is severe inefficiency due to poorly paid teachers being absent in order to work on their own farms or at other jobs. In such cases the private sector may be able to enter the market and supply cheap, though fee-paying, education for the poor. An example is Kenya where some public funding is put into establishing schools through community enterprise, but where parents are expected to pay fees for the running costs of the establishment. A very small proportion of local taxation is thus used for education, but in reality parents meet a considerable proportion of student costs. In other countries, such as China, the schools have become entrepreneurial in raising funds by providing agricultural, industrial or technological services. Even in developed countries schools appear to need to raise additional funds either through parental donations, or by hiring out school facilities when they are not otherwise in use. New Zealand schools are encouraged to recruit overseas pupils who live with local families and bring with them both enhanced pupil fees and a boost to local income.

The World Bank has advocated that parents pay fees in both state and private schools in developing countries in order to increase the number of places. While such policies probably increase efficiency by expanding educational provision, the downside is increased inequity as poor parents are less likely to send their children to school. By contrast, most educational provision in Eastern Europe is funded through disbursement at local level from a direct grant to the area from central government and few parents would expect to pay for any element of their children's basic education.

There is a much weaker argument for free provision of higher education than there is for free provision of basic education. The argument is that the return to higher education is mainly private, not public, and therefore the individual should pay most of the costs. Furthermore, if higher education is subsidised, the people who benefit are middle-class households whose children have a much greater participation rate in higher education than children from poorer households, and future graduates who earn higher than average incomes. Yet the people who pay taxes include large numbers of people on average or below-average incomes. A subsidy to higher education is therefore regressive as money flows from the less well-off to the better-off. This is the essence of the case for students paying fees for higher education and taking out student loans to pay for fees and living costs while in full-time education (Barr and Crawford 2005).

The sources of funding for education

Releasing public resources for education usually requires public recognition of likely gains of spending on education rather than from expenditure on other public services. This leads to key policy questions at international, national and institutional level. At international level, the debate is one of establishing priorities. At the national level, Tony Blair's objective on his election as prime minister in the UK in 1997 was 'education, education, education'. At the local level, and depending upon the governmental framework, there are different demands for locally raised revenues leading to competition between support for schools or for social housing or for support of the elderly. At the institutional level, there is very rarely sufficient funding for intended plans, and so scarce resources have to be allocated in the most efficient and effective way possible. In most countries, the public sector is not the only provider. However limited their incomes, families have the opportunity to use private wealth for their own ends, and if people believe that public education provision is limited, they can support it by supplementary funding of public schools, or by supporting entirely private institutions. Policy questions arise from differing views on the desirable balance between private and public funding and the ways in which overall provision can be secured.

Public expenditure on education (or any other service) is financed mainly through taxation. This may come entirely from central government using revenues from a centralised collection system, or from local funding, usually by a local rate precept, or by a combination of the two systems. Other sources are revenues earned by the sale of goods, services or assets by public sector organisations, as in the sale of expert services by university departments and borrowing by the public sector, usually for buildings and other capital projects, although ultimately this has to be paid for via taxation or state revenues.

There is very great variation in the way in which national systems, and even local arrangements, resource education. There will be a combination of funding from basic sources, generally from central government, local government, the community and fee payments, supported by central and government special bidding, parental support and sponsorship of various types.

For the private sector, the most common source of revenue is that of fee payments, with some very limited additional support from public sources. Many such private schools, colleges and universities in the historically developed world are supported by large endowments that have accrued over the years and which have been more or less skilfully invested to yield current income. They may also be aided by charitable foundations and, in some instances, by services rendered, for example, during school vacations.

Public and private provision and efficiency and equity in resource use

Efficient use of public funding requires that the agencies to whom funding is delegated, be it a district who then allocates funds to schools, or be it directly to the school or college, yields both technical and productive efficiency. To assist this, leadership at district or institutional level has to recognise the ways in which national objectives can be attained and provide the necessary supervision to ensure results. The 'immediacy of responsibility' principle applies in that if local funds are being used, those responsible at local level are accountable to their community and will be more likely to be efficient, than if their funding comes from distant central government to whom they are responsible by occasional supervision, inspection or audit. It could be argued that the combination of central and local funding that supports schools in many countries offers a combination of central supervision with local accountability – except when central government elections are imminent.

Efficiency within the private sector is dependent upon the management at each institution. However, there are broader questions about the capability of the private sector to contribute to the national educational good in an efficient way if it is funded at a higher level beyond basic provision and without the constraints of public sector institutions. Nationally, it may be asked whether the use of private investment in this way is efficient – how much greater would outputs and outcomes be if the public sector was supported at the same level?

In the public provision of education, equity is compromised where there is no universally consistent source of funding to meet varying socio-economic conditions. Equity issues also arise when it appears that privately funded provision offers a quality of education not available in the public sector.

Conclusion

This chapter has introduced the criteria by which resource allocation can be judged. It has considered the outputs and outcomes of education and shown how these are used in assessing the private and the public benefits accruing from education. The debate is whether public or private investment in education is more productive in given contexts. In brief, the advantage of central government funding is that of equity and also in ensuring greater national uniformity in standards when education is regarded as a national and not a local public good. As governments have been increasingly concerned with the importance of the education sector in producing a highly skilled labour force, so tolerance of differential standards has diminished. In order to compensate in those areas where deprivation in many forms inhibits educational outputs and outcomes, fiscal equalisation has been increasingly used, either by supplementary central or local public funding, to enhance educational effectiveness. This suggests that many educational problems can be solved simply by a higher level of resourcing, but there is increasing evidence – as shown in the management data in OFSTED reports in the UK – that without good resource allocation aimed at the fulfilment of stated educational objectives, spending more does not necessarily achieve a better educational output.

3 The allocation of public finance to education

In this chapter we will:

- examine the sources of public funding of education (central, local and institutional level);
- distinguish between the level of government that provides funding and the level that determines how it is used;
- examine the advantages and disadvantages of central and local funding of education;
- examine different methods of allocating public funding;
- assess the advantages and disadvantages of different types of funding with regard to efficiency and equity.

Public funding of education

We have already demonstrated that there is considerable variation in the resources made available for education from public funds. This can be attributed to the source, the allocation rules applying to resources, and conditionality.

Source

The finance for publicly funded education may come directly from central government which raises the resources needed for national services through direct and indirect taxation and then allocates the funds to educational organisations in different ways. Alternatively, the funds may come from local taxation – usually related to property values – but also from local direct taxation. The situation, however, is made more complex where local authorities act as agents for school resourcing and where they are supported by funds from central government to which they add locally raised revenues.

The balance in the proportion of funding from central and local government varies from country to country and changes over time. Higher education funding is usually paid directly from central government to universities whereas most basic primary education is funded from local authorities that have varying amounts of central government grants to support their activities. If a local area wishes to make provision beyond the basic level it can only do so by raising local revenues – and some areas are more able and willing to do this than others. The increasing decentralisation of control of school administration has resulted in schools being free to enhance their basic funding through locally raised support.

Allocation principles

These affect the way in which funds are distributed to schools and colleges. As we will discuss later, these funds may be distributed according to formulas containing indicators, such as the numbers and age of students attending a particular school or group of schools. Another method is by matching payments, for example, when central government matches local area funding by a set ratio. An alternative is bidding, by which a school or group of schools can put up a bid for funding to meet particular needs, for example, for those with special educational requirements, or submit cost estimates for their entire budget.

Conditionality

This arises when funding is subject to the school or group of schools meeting central or local government requirements, for example, by teaching according to approved methods or to an approved curriculum. Grants with conditions attached to them are called categorical, specific or earmarked. If the provider of funding does not impose conditions on how the recipient uses the funding, it is a block grant.

For and against central or local funding of education

There is considerable policy debate on the appropriate mix of local and central government funding of education. In part this division is determined by long-standing constitutional settlements. Where these define a federal state, as in Germany, the USA, Canada and Australia, for example, the vast majority of education funding is determined at state level. The state can then decide to be the sole provider of public education funding or to leave a considerable amount of fund-raising to local school districts. Elsewhere, for example, in the Scandinavian countries, there is a long tradition of the importance of local community government. So in Sweden over 70 per cent of education funding is spent by municipalities. In England, by contrast, it used to be 25 per cent until 2006, when the level of local general spending on education became entirely determined by central government through a 100 per cent dedicated schools grant.

The mix of local and central funding can be very varied. The main dimensions along which variations occur are:

- the extent to which general education is partly funded directly by local government and partly directly by central government;

- a split of resourcing responsibility between local and central governments, for example, a common split is central government paying for staff and local government paying for non-staff items;

- the extent to which education is funded out of local taxation or central government grants to local authorities, rather than direct grants from central government to schools;

- the conditions central government attaches to grants to local governments.

We will now discuss the advantages and disadvantages of local and central government funding of education, focusing on three models of financing arrangements, which highlight the main advantages and disadvantages of central versus local financing.

Model 1: fully funded by local government

In this model educational institutions are fully funded by local government out of local tax revenues. These usually include local property tax and, in addition, may consist of sales taxes or even a local income tax. The local authority can also borrow on the capital market to fund capital projects. The advantage of this model is that it promotes external efficiency because local people can decide on local levels of education spending and taxation to support it. This was argued initially by Tiebout (1956) and so is known as the Tiebout model. Here households can obtain their preferred mix of local public goods by moving to the jurisdiction that best matches their preferences. Consumers' satisfaction or utility is thus maximised so the criterion of external efficiency is met by these arrangements. Locally raised taxes and borrowing also encourages direct democracy, as in Swiss cantons and US school districts, where votes are cast for specific expenditure proposals. The Tiebout model is also likely to promote internal efficiency, as local people are able to ensure that tax revenues they have supplied are used efficiently.

The vital premise upon which local funding of collective goods maximises social welfare is that these goods are all local public goods. This means that the public benefit from, say education, is shared only by the residents of the jurisdiction and with an immobile population does not spill over to other areas and so affect outsiders.

It therefore follows that this argument in favour of local funding and local provision gets weaker as the collective good in question cannot be confined to one area because of population mobility, and so what occurs in one district has wider spillover effects to the rest of the nation. This applies particularly to education. With globalisation, governments have become increasingly concerned about the importance of a well-educated labour force to enable effective competition on international markets. Fifty or more years ago school-level education could be regarded as a local public good in developed countries, since there was work for unskilled labour in industries that were then less mechanised and less technologically advanced. As governments have taken a more active interest in the quality of education nationwide, they have encroached, as far as political conditions allow, on local government freedoms to run education according to local preferences.

Another disadvantage of the Tiebout model is that it promotes horizontal inequality across the nation and diminishes social cohesion. With people grouping themselves into local communities in accordance with their preferences for public goods and tax rates, there will be great differences in the amount spent per head in different areas. Wealthier areas will spend more per head and have better services if they so choose. Poor people would find tax rates high in high-spending areas and move to localities where less tax revenue is collected and less is spent, with consequently lower quality education.

A good example of great differences in per student expenditure for general education are the cantons in Bosnia and Herzegovina, shown in Figure 3.1. The political settlement that ended the civil war in 1995 established 13 local government jurisdictions of greatly varying size, each with its own tax-raising capacity. The absence of national accord had, up until 2003, prevented the establishment of any tax redistribution. The level of spending in each jurisdiction, therefore, was determined by the amount of local tax revenues.

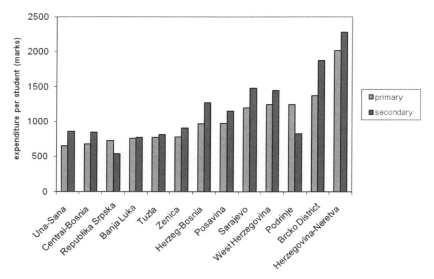

Figure 3.1   Expenditure per student for primary and secondary schools in Bosnia and Herzegovina (2002) by jurisdiction

(From: Levačić 2003: Table 6)

Consequently expenditure per student was three times greater in the highest compared to the lowest spending area.

The effect of different local priorities may be that education is favoured in an area where there are many younger people but less so in an area where the demographic balance differs and older people exert greater pressure for social and health services. Within a local area the policy and decision-makers are usually well known and the possibility of lobbying either officially or in private may result in decisions that favour one organisation at the expense of another. Where the disbursement is managed at the local level, the possibility of administrative malpractice, or simply favouring one head who is known to have 'influence in high places', may also result in inequalities. As a result there will be considerable differences in the level of provision within areas of a single country and this may lead to population migration in order to secure the services required. Such instability then puts the favoured local area under pressure and, while political theorists argue that this will prompt improvement in the area from which movement has occurred, this is by no means certain.

Model 2: local determination of spending with fiscal equalisation

The inequity in local ability to raise tax revenues to fund local services can be removed by fiscal equalisation in which tax revenues are redistributed from areas with high tax bases to areas with low tax bases. This can be organised by central government, as in the UK, or by local governments, as in Sweden. The Tiebout model's advantage in terms of external efficiency is preserved because local governments receive a block grant to even out the playing field but can then choose their own level of spending on individual services as well as decide how much extra to raise in local taxes. However, the disadvantage of having a national public good subject to local preferences and hence differences in levels and quality of provision remains. Whether public resources are advantageously used to secure efficiency and equity is a matter for local organisational determination. But this is the inevitable price of local discretion and local democratic decision-making. This model is accompanied by considerable political bargaining between local and central government, if the latter is the provider of block grants. This may lead to a situation where central government politicians attempt to put the needs of their locality before the national good (known as pork barrel politics) as they seek to buy local political support. One feature of developing countries is that the central area in and near the capital tends to have better resourced schools even when funding comes from central government grants. Azerbaijan and Ghana are examples.

To operate equitably and transparently, central government funding of local government requires well-managed administrative systems with good accountability relationships. This is often not present in developing countries. As World Bank public expenditure tracking surveys have shown, a high proportion, especially of non-salary funding, has not reached schools – Uganda is an example. In developing countries with poor tax bases and weak administration of revenue and expenditure flows, fiscal equalisation is not feasible. By default, a high proportion of school resourcing is left to local communities to fund, with consequent inadequacy and inequality.

Model 3: central government determined funding

Horizontal inequality and national preferences for education as a national public good are secured if central government determines the amount of funding received by schools and allocates it on the basis of an equitable formula that takes into account differences is spending need. The role of local government, if it has any, is to manage the distribution of funding and the education services for which it has responsibility. These will be limited if schools have a high level of financial delegation. The disadvantage of this model is that national uniformity disregards differences in local tastes for public goods and therefore may harm external efficiency. Without a large service such as education to be managed, there are fewer incentives and opportunities for local democratic decision-making. Extreme centralisation is avoided if financial management responsibilities are substantially delegated to a school council comprised of local community representatives. However, there is likely to be conformity to national standards and hence limited scope for local self-determination on educational matters.

Models: summary

In short, as we showed in the previous chapter, there is a balance to be struck between central and local funding. Most countries use a combination of both with four main objectives:

- to ensure basic levels of provision by providing a minimum amount of central funding which is then 'topped up' by local taxation;

- to promote specific projects which central government wants implemented in addition to standard provision through direct central grants;

- to ensure equity between local jurisdictions by providing each with an equivalent amount to provide for local needs, after adjusting for differences in need and in ability to raise local tax;

- to create opportunities for the local community members to be involved so that differences in local needs and preferences can be addressed.

In some countries the system becomes yet more complex because central or local government may provide a basic level of funding for educational resources but then allow, or encourage, schools to seek some support from their community through sponsorship or fee payment. Complexity is increased where central funding meets certain types of expenditure, such as teaching staff at a stated ratio rate, but where local funding is necessary to provide buildings and non-teaching staff, and school funding is sought through parent and teacher money-raising activities to meet the costs of books and equipment, as is the case in Kenya. Accountability is more difficult and layers of supervisory staffing more likely to occur.

Types of central government grant

Grants from central government take varied forms. This is because they have to satisfy different objectives and can be used to secure particular policy implementation. There are three main dimensions to providing central financing for schools and colleges, which are whether or not the grant is:

- a block grant (also lump sum) or a categorical grant;

- a matching or closed grant;

- determined by formula or by bidding.

Block (lump sum) or categorical grants

Block grants (also called lump sum grants) are made to a local authority without any specific conditions being imposed as to their use. They allow freedom at local government or at school or college level and may promote a particular response to the needs of the community, for example, by allowing a rural school to concentrate on agricultural education while allowing a school in an urban area to develop specialisations that meet local industrial needs. Because these are generally non-specific payments, the process of resource planning, implementation and evaluation is likely to be left to the school or college, although audit systems will usually seek to secure value for money. As block grants can be used according to local preferences, needs and costs, they tend to promote efficiency.

The opposite to a block grant is a categorical grant – also called a specific or earmarked grant – which central government requires are used for specific purposes: for example, to support teachers' professional development, or to purchase computers or textbooks. Governments that practise historic funding and pay grants according to the number of staff are also using categorical funding, though the category is a broad one. This is a very typical practice in transition states. Some, like Azerbaijan, practise an extreme form of categorical funding in which the Ministry of Finance allocates precise sums to a very large number of budget lines (for example, staff; stationery; domestic travel, such as hotel expenses; water; gas; etc.) and permits no switching between lines without central approval. Such detailed and inflexible categorical grants tend to encourage internal inefficiency. However, some categorical grants that support particular projects, which are perceived accurately by central government to increase educational performance, would promote efficiency. Categorical grants that ensure equal national standards of provision promote horizontal equity.

Matching (or closed) grants

A matching grant is one where the money the local school or college receives from central government is dependent on how much it spends. The grant could be for a widely defined purpose, such as education, or for much more narrowly defined projects that the government wishes to promote. In effect, a matching grant makes the items it is used to purchase cheaper to the local unit, because for every £1 they spend, they get a fraction X in grant. It is this reduction in relative price that encourages the local unit to spend on the items for which a matching grant is available.

Matching grants are used to stimulate local mobilisation of revenues and promote efficiency by ensuring local people want the expenditure. This system releases funds for a local- or school-based project on the basis of matching the revenue raised locally, either through local government, or from the community or other sponsorship, with a central government 'top up'. This may vary from a very small central element to support local community building efforts in Kenya, to a very large element such as the establishment of specialist schools in England and Wales where the community has been required to raise up to 5 per cent of a plan for technological improvement in order to release 95 per cent of government funding over a four-year period. The advantage is that the school will secure support for its aims and objectives, but the disadvantage is that it will have to conform to government requirements if the funding is to be made available.

Formula or bid allocation

All the grants discussed above can be affected by the way in which they are calculated. A formula for allocation is a defined set of indicators, each with a cash allocation, that is the same for all grant recipients in a given category. Common indicators for a funding formula are the numbers of students meeting criteria such as age, social deprivation (free meals or uniform) or special educational needs. Formulas can be varied in order to meet national objectives, for example, by supporting nursery education more generously than other sectors. These formulas may be applied according to a number of criteria. Income and socially contingent but non-specific grants may be made where schools are deprived because local revenue levels are insufficient to meet needs. Supplementary funds may be allocated, dependent upon markers of deprivation, such as housing conditions, numbers of single parent families, ethnic mix, unemployment statistics and so on.

Alternatively, the decision on whether to allocate funding at all to the local school or college and how much to allocate can be decided through bidding processes. These are used to encourage schools and colleges to develop their own approaches to particular areas of development and to enable central government to allocate limited funding to those projects it thinks will make the best use of the grant money. This kind of funding is used to encourage pedagogic change or to secure the introduction of information and communications technology. It has also been used as a means of securing development through international funding. This is seen in the work of the World Bank where educational development projects have been encouraged by schools bidding for improvement grants, for example, in Bosnia and Herzegovina.

The disadvantage of bidding is the amount of time it takes applicants to make a bid, especially if it is rejected, with consequent loss of morale. This is worsened for resource leaders when it becomes obvious that only schools in certain contexts are able to secure support or where the bid allocation system appears to be favouring areas where it is important to secure political support. Bidding arrangements of this sort are often dependent on cumbersome evaluation procedures and resultant administrative inefficiency. The gains are that change is encouraged, cutting edge planning is facilitated (if well-judged value-for-money projects are invested in) and those organisations securing aid develop heightened self-esteem.

Grants: summary

Grants from central government can take varied forms that draw upon all three dimensions. This is because they are aimed at satisfying different objectives and can be used to secure particular policy implementation. Therefore, it is possible to have a non-categorical matched grant allocated by formula (for example, number of pupils).

As the above discussion indicates, the criteria by which resources are allocated to individual schools or universities are important for the efficiency incentives they signal to educational managers and for their equity implications (see the example below). The use of formulas for allocating a 'global' budget to schools (based mainly on the number and ages of its pupils) has become more widespread. As Ross and Levačić (1999) argue, a properly constructed formula can encourage both efficiency in resource use, horizontal equity (the same amount spent per similar student) and vertical equity (differential amounts per student, depending on indicators of social and educational need).

Bosnia and Herzegovina provides a good example of how resourcing practices can cause inefficiency due to inflexibility.

After the war of 1992–5, which halved national income per head and from which the newly independent country was only slowly recovering, schools faced great difficulties in operating efficiently and with adequate resources. The inevitable shortage of funding was exacerbated by the system of resource allocation. There was a rigid formula for allocating both teaching and support staff according to the number of classes the school had. Staff were paid directly by the local authority. Schools received very small and irregular amounts for non-staff expenses. As a consequence, schools were poorly maintained and had few books and little equipment.

Heating bills were paid directly by the local authority so there was no incentive for schools to use energy efficiently. Schools were overstaffed, especially with non-teaching staff. Headteachers and school councils could not choose a more efficient pattern of resource use because they could not switch funding between staff and non-staff expenditures. Small but expensive schools could not be closed because there was no provision in the budget for switching the money saved on staff to pay for transporting pupils to a different school. International consultants recommended a switch to per pupil funding so that schools would receive a global budget that could be flexibly allocated between the different resource needs as judged by headteachers and school councils. So far this has been only partially implemented in some districts.

Applying the criteria to allocation systems

In Chapter 2 an outline was given of the criteria by which the use of educational resources can be judged. The varying demand for education is manifest in different ways and met through a combination of central, local and cost-sharing methods. It is important for educational leaders to apply judgement when using criteria in that they need to be aware of the ways in which they can argue for enhanced or changed systems of allocation.

To remind you briefly of definitions: efficiency is maximising educational outputs given the resources available, effectiveness is a judgement of the extent to which objectives are met (value for money is achieved by both efficiency and effectiveness) and equity is the allocation of resources in a socially fair manner. This is illustrated in Table 3.1 below showing how the criteria for resource allocation and evaluation may be applied to primary education in Luxembourg. It demonstrates the complexity of funding at commune, canton and

Table 3.1 Funding arrangements for primary education in Luxembourg

Element	Funding	Context	Efficiency	Effectiveness	Equity
Primary education – buildings	District level	Aim for primary class sizes of 25 pupils. Communes urged to co-operate to secure maximum use of premises.	Build within a set of standards to be eligible for central government grants.	Centralised inspectoral system applies audit procedures to building use in adjoining communes.	Additional funding for communes with low population density and isolated communities.
Primary education – staffing	Centrally by application of pupil–staff ratio.	Commune amalgamation to ensure classes of near ratio size 1:25.	Ratio use ensures that basic needs are met. Communes may pay for more staff.	Inspectoral system checks that staff are providing value for money.	Schools in areas of social deprivation or with high 'new worker' responsibility have an improved ratio.

national levels (even in such a small country). Each element that is differently funded can be considered against the criteria of efficiency in using funding, effectiveness in securing objectives, and equity in providing according to local need.

Table 3.1 shows the general principles and systems that are used to ensure that funds are properly allocated in accordance with national and local resource control policies in Luxembourg. However, to judge whether resources are being used effectively or efficiently requires rather more financial detail than the table suggests – for example, if two adjoining communes purchase additional staff to work with a small number of children in each of two schools, this may not be the most efficient use of resourcing compared to sharing the teachers between the two schools or employing them in one amalgamated school.

Some of the grants made for educational resourcing are allocated by applying formulas, for example, by giving a per capita payment for each student in an area or school. A refinement is to ascertain the actual needs of each student if they are to achieve their potential and then use this as the basis of formula development. This is known as needs-based allocation because it tempers allocation in the light of social and educational contextual issues to secure equity of opportunity. Researchers have looked at the way in which countries reconcile educational resourcing and policy development through formula and needs-based approaches. The criteria discussed above can be linked up with the agreed social, political and cultural aims of national life by using the framework of values suggested by Swanson and King (1991: 183). These values are:

- liberty (offering choice and diversity in educational provision);

- equality (offering similar opportunities for all to access educational resources);

- fraternity (offering social cohesiveness despite the context of a school or college);

- efficiency (the achievement of the highest outputs for a given set of inputs);

- economic growth (through the application of educational standards).

Conclusion

This chapter has examined approaches to the allocation of funds for education at central and local levels. Systems vary in their underlying political philosophy as well as in their degree of local autonomy, in their capacity to raise funds for educational purposes, and in the degree of control at all levels. Where public funding is limited it is also likely that private capacity to support education will be limited, but schools and colleges may seek this support to supplement or fulfil their needs. Leaders and managers in these institutions have to be aware of their funding systems so that they can encourage public pressure where there is inadequacy or inequity. In those countries where there is a significant degree of devolved funding, the responsibility for efficiency and effectiveness, and hence value for money, rests with them. In the next chapter we consider the need for awareness of cost structures.

4 Cost structures in education

In this chapter we will:

- explain why it is necessary to analyse education costs;
- offer definitions of cost terms (such as opportunity cost, variable/fixed, direct/indirect, total/average/marginal);
- explain cost attribution and unit costing;
- show the use of costs in assessing value for money.

Why it is important to know about costs

It is important that those responsible for managing the use of resources in education know how much those resources cost. Think for a moment about the costs of two teachers in the same school. Are they paid the same salary? Are they allowed to undertake the same training away from school? Do they need the same classroom equipment to undertake their teaching work? Does one cost more than the other because they have a poor absence record? Is a female teacher likely to need maternity leave?, and so on.

Simkins (2000) argues that allocating resources effectively is only possible if those making decisions know exactly how much the various elements of staffing, buildings and teaching materials actually cost. This is necessary because:

- Public resources for education are scarce and therefore it is important that they are well used. Knowledge of costs enables comparing alternative ways of achieving objectives so as to select the most efficient.

- If revenues have to be obtained from marketing educational services, then it is essential to know what must be charged in order to cover costs.

- The trend towards self-managing institutions means that as the purchasers of goods and services, schools and colleges need to have full information about the costs of the resources they purchase and use.

- Centralised monitoring of self-managing institutions requires that schools and colleges pay attention to costs as one of the means of comparison to ensure value for money.

- Transparency and accountability: by quantifying the costs of all resources used, it is possible to demonstrate the effects of their use and to assess whether the expenditure offers value for money.

Even though these purposes exist beyond the institution, it is necessary to use cost analysis within the school or college in a forward-looking way (for example, by using cost estimates) in order to make decisions about the future use of resources. It is necessary to use information on actual costs retrospectively to check that expenditure has taken place in accordance with what was planned, and to evaluate past expenditures for value for money. Berne and Stiefel (1995) show that whether looking forward or retrospectively, cost information illuminates understanding of the production function that determines the relationship between the inputs to education and outputs in the form of pupil attainment. This informs managers about the relationship between the additional resources allocated to a school or programme and additional achievement. Such analysis also provides information on comparative cost-effectiveness to establish whether one pattern of expenditure is more or less effective than another. The use of data for comparison stresses that resources can be used in alternative ways – to do one thing may be at the cost of doing something else.

Opportunity costs

Resources are almost always scarce: it is rare to have such an abundance of resources that no more are required. When resources are limited, we have to make choices and face opportunity costs. The cost of choosing to do one thing is what we can't do as a result of that choice. The opportunity cost of using a set of resources is the forgone benefits of the next best alternative use of those resources. If there were no financial constraints on education and school organisers were able to use as many staff as they wished, in buildings that imposed no constraints and with as much equipment as subject teaching demanded, there would be no need for concern about costs. Most schools can only purchase more of one item, say staff, if they purchase less of another. An example illustrates this.

Mulawaru School in a growing suburban area in East Africa has 120 students aged 11–14, organised in three classes with the headteacher and three staff. A central government grant funds basic building provision and a modest fee income from parents meets most other expenses. The headteacher has attempted to maintain a staffing ratio of 1:40 and is available to support class teachers, teach smaller groups in basic subjects and to cope with administration – defined as 'fund-rasing and working with the local community'. Because of these efforts and recruitment to the stated maximum for the school, he has been able to enhance the termly income so that another half-time member of staff can be employed or the money used in different ways. The alternatives are many and varied for a school with so many needs. The headteacher believes that an additional half-time member of staff would be beneficial because the part-timer could ensure that small group work was undertaken on a regular basis to support both those pupils seeking admission to a high school as well as those with special learning needs. The teachers favour continuing as they are, but purchasing new furniture to give every child a desk, up-to-date textbooks and some basic computer equipment that will offer all pupils a chance to understand new technology. The parents would like the money to be used to service a loan so that toilet facilities could be extended; members of the local community council also favour this option, but also believe that additional catering facilities would enable the school to do much more for the adult community and those pupils with long daily journeys to and from school. The district inspectors have reported that the school was not using existing resources wisely with the headteacher and teachers spending so much of their time on administration and maintenance of the buildings and they recommended that any additional staffing should be used to ensure a greater degree of non-teaching support. Pressures are also growing from local parents who want to get their children into the school and the government has agreed to fund the building of another classroom if satisfactory staffing arrangements can be made to ensure improved educational outcomes.

The underlying principle for evaluating any additional funding is that of opportunity cost. In economic analysis, the value of resources is measured in terms of the alternative opportunities that are given up in order to spend resources in a particular way. The opportunity cost of building a new school may well be the loss of a local hospital, or the provision of new buildings for community purposes. At local level, curriculum provision may be affected by the same principle.

The cost of half a teacher is the amount of the salary released that could be used for one or more of several alternatives – the money cost of purchasing x rather than y. It is also necessary to consider the implications of undertaking different courses of action – the educational costs. Think of the loss to those children who would have benefited from one-to-one teaching if the decision is taken to use released funds to rebuild the school kitchen. In the UK, central government has funded and trained staff for a numeracy hour and a literacy hour in all primary schools. The opportunity cost is the benefit of using these resources in another way, such as developing pupils' creativity. However, as in the example above, it is often impossible to measure the alternative forgone benefits. Consequently opportunity costs are often evaluated in terms of the market prices of the resources; for example, the hours of teacher time are costed in terms of the amount of salary paid for this time. Headteachers and teachers must use their professional judgement to determine which of several alternative uses of resources, as in the case of Muluwaru School, will yield the most benefit.

There is a distinction to be made between the opportunity cost to a school or college and that to society as a whole. An example of this arises when a school has a categorical grant that has to be spent, for example, on a minority ethnic achievement teacher. This post is either filled or not and the money cannot be diverted, so this has no opportunity cost to the school. However, there is a loss to society because resources allocated for support to individuals are not being used. This loss can only be avoided if the funds not spent at the school are returned to central government to be used in another way.

There can be 'hidden' opportunity costs; for example, land given by a village community for a new building may not have any immediate alternative use but this could change with revised planning laws. The time given by parents to prepare an environmental study area is not directly measurable, and the computer resources given by a local company would only have an opportunity cost if commercial sales were possible. Additionally, managers often ignore the opportunity cost of using resources that have already been paid for – this applies particularly to aspects of the use of staff time. The opportunity cost of staff spending time in meetings is often not appreciated by managers.

Sunk costs

Sunk costs (Rosenbaum and Lamort 1992) are costs that need to be incurred to take advantage of some opportunity (for example, sinking a mine before you can extract gold) and which cannot be recovered once incurred – hence they are sunk. They are non-recoverable since once they are incurred there is no longer an opportunity cost, since the resources cannot be sold to anyone else as they have no other use.

Creative use of space within schools means that there are few truly sunk costs, but they do happen. For example, the installation of modern language teaching laboratories in schools as part of a national development programme in the UK incurred sunk costs for schools during the 1970s and 1980s. The teaching approach was short-lived, and so until schools were able to raise funds for alternative adaptations, many laboratories lay idle.

Differentiating between types of cost

Cost consciousness is inexact and often subjective if the impact of a course of action is described in general terms. Budget consciousness is much more exact, but giving monetary value to resources requires understanding a range of cost concepts. Several classification systems apply to costs and are used in economic commentary. It is possible to think about the same item of expenditure in different ways:

- Recurrent costs (sometimes called current costs) are those that have to be met year after year, for example, teachers' salaries, stationery, fuel compared with capital costs, which are those used to purchase durable assets, such as buildings.

- Direct costs are those that can be attributed to a particular activity, such as the costs of running a science lesson, including staff, teaching and equipment compared with indirect costs, which are incurred to keep a school (or business) running, but which cannot be attributed directly to specific activities like courses. They include running costs of the buildings, management and administration costs, and central services, such as the library.

- Variable costs are those that increase according to the volume of activity in schools and colleges, which is directly related to the number of students (for example, if the pupil–teacher ratio is 1:30 and there are 90 students, then the variable cost is that of three teachers) compared with fixed costs that have to be met irrespective of the number of students in the school (for example, buildings, advisory services and administration).

- Total costs arise by aggregating all the cost factors in the educational enterprise at whatever management level it operates (for example, within a school or a district). From these, by dividing the total costs by the number of students involved, it is possible to define the average costs that arise from educating one pupil or student (there are times when reference may be made to per class average figures).

It is a common misunderstanding that direct and variable costs are the same and that fixed and indirect costs are also the same. They are distinct concepts. Variable and fixed costs are economics concepts, while direct and indirect costs are accounting concepts. Let us consider the example of expanding a school by a class of 25 students. The direct costs are the additional teaching time and learning materials per student, since we can directly attribute these costs to the extra students. However, we also know that the 25 students will use the library and create more work for the librarian, even though the school will not hire any more librarian time. The book stock will wear out a bit more rapidly, but the exact amount and additional cost of this cannot be precisely known. For an economist, these are variable costs. For an accountant, they are indirect costs because they have to be attributed to the extra students in some relatively arbitrary way. This requires using some measure of the volume of activity or output. In a school, this volume would be numbers of pupils or numbers of lesson and homework hours. Thus an indirect library cost per student or lesson hour could be arrived at.

For accountancy purposes, fixed costs would also be attributed as indirect costs to each unit of output or, in the case of schools, students. So the fixed cost of the headteacher's salary, which does not change when 25 more students enter the school, would be divided by 25 more students in order to arrive at the indirect cost per student to central management.

Over time all costs can become variable. When planners estimate the cost of a new school, all inputs, including buildings, are variable. When applying cost concepts to estimate costs for decision-making, it is necessary to use considerable judgement over what it is appropriate to include. This is illustrated by the following example.

A local health advisory group in a depressed area of Johannesburg, South Africa, wanted to run a training course so that 'health helpers' could work within their area. The local high school was prepared to help, but insisted that the costs of the course should be met in full. The calculation of costs was an interesting debate in itself and problems included:

- The accommodation offered was one room with electricity and water, but as another room in the school would be open for an evening academic class, what would be the further accommodation costs of running the course?

- The teaching would be provided by a member of the health team, but the science element of the course required that the day school science teacher also needed to attend as a demonstrator. Should she be paid at the full rate for evening work even though she was only an assistant for much of the time?

- The class members were required to provide their own stationery, but they were allowed to use the school textbooks for the two academic components – science and psychology. What would be a fair repayment to the school for this facility?

- Should there be a payment to the school administration fund for the use of the photocopier for worksheets that would be required in weeks four and six of the course?

- What would be a fair payment to the district administration for the supervision provided by the adult evening organiser?

The complexities of arriving at a calculated sum were such that the school principal suggested that the time taken to work out an appropriate figure was out of proportion to the gain likely to be made. This offers an excellent example of opportunity cost at work.

Levin and McEwan (2001) demonstrate further the problems in securing full information as the basis of costing an enterprise. They suggest that some costs may be hidden (for example, the general value of being able to use a building); that some large maintenance costs (for example, a new heating system) should be shared across a number of years; that the unit being analysed may be aggregated into figures for the organisation as a whole, and that it may be necessary to incorporate expenditure on external factors (for example, road safety). They offer the *ingredients method*, which is concerned only with the costs of educational intervention, including:

- personnel (salaries, on costs and time worked);
- training of personnel;
- facilities;
- equipment and materials;
- other inputs, for example, travel, school uniforms.

In all the calculations of costs, it is necessary to define exactly what is meant by each 'ingredient', to quantify each ingredient (for example, per teacher hour) and to establish the cost or price per unit.

Average and marginal costs

Average costs are the total costs of a school or college or course membership, divided by the number of pupils, undergraduates or members. Sometimes the total may be divided by hours or course or outcomes, such as successful course completion. For some purposes, however, it is necessary to know the cost incurred in making provision for one extra person. This is the marginal cost.

Because some costs are fixed (for example, some part of a school's management costs and buildings costs), average costs will fall at first as the number of students increases. Average costs could eventually level out and remain constant as student numbers increase or they could eventually rise as more students are enrolled. If the average cost curve is U-shaped (as depicted in economics textbooks), then the marginal cost will be equal to average cost when average cost is at its minimum.

When average cost is at its minimum, average and marginal costs are the same. This is the point at which all resources are being used in the most efficient way because the cost per student is at its lowest possible point. However, it may well not be practicable to run a school at just this size, if the demand for places is greater and the extra revenue from additional students covers their additional costs. Alternatively, in sparsely populated areas with poor transport facilities, it may be necessary to run small schools even though the average costs are greater than they would be for a larger school.

The marginal cost of educating one more student is an important consideration when deciding whether to expand or not. Schools and universities have a marginal cost 'curve' shaped like a step. If the classes joined by the additional student are not full, then there is no need to employ another teacher and so the marginal cost is small (for example, only additional textbooks and materials). However, once the class is full, an extra student can only be admitted by splitting the class in two and employing an extra teacher, which raises marginal cost at this point quite steeply.

Case study 1: Costing example: setting up a nursery class

A steep rise in marginal costs is illustrated in the costing for nursery classes in an English primary school. The school has space to accommodate up to 40 3 to 5-year-old children. Regulations require a 1:13 adult to child ratio and that a qualified teacher must be present. For a class size of 13 children, only a nursery teacher will be employed; for 26 children, a nursery nurse will be employed as well, and for 39 children, a teaching assistant would be added to the staff. The staff costs are given below in Table 4.1, where the total staff cost is shown in the right-hand column. The marginal cost of staff shoots up when the class rises from 13 to 14 (nursery nurse employed) and from 26 to 27 (teaching assistant employed). Otherwise marginal staff costs are zero.

Table 4.1 Staffing costs for 13, 26 and 39 children

	Cost of staff member	13 children	26 children	39 children	Total cost of staff
Teacher	£23,288	1	1	1	£23,288
Nursery nurse	£11,571	0	1	1	£34,859
Teaching assistant	£9,722	0	0	1	£44,581

The non-staff costs are shown in Table 4.2. Materials worth £300 have to be bought to start the class and thereafter £5 needs to be spent per child.

The other costs are the indirect costs of running the school building and administering the school. For the whole school these come to £43,846. Since the nursery will occupy 12 per cent of the school's space, 12 per cent of these indirect costs are attributed to the nursery, which is £5,264.

Table 4.2   Non-staff costs

Materials and equipment	£300
Plus £5 per child thereafter	
Facilities: indirect costs	
Repairs and maintenance	£6,000
Ground maintenance	£1,350
Energy and water	£3,700
Caretaker and cleaning	£13,490
Administrative staff	£12,349
Administration: services	£6,975
Total	£43,864
Apportioned to nursery at 12% of total school space	£5,264

The problem for the school is to decide whether it is worthwhile to open the nursery class. If it does, it will get a fixed block grant of £10,000 from its local authority plus £1,000 per year for each full-time nursery child. It therefore needs to compare the average revenue it would get with the average variable costs. The indirect costs can be ignored on the assumption that these are not affected by whether the nursery class is run. Following data in Table 4.1 and its graphical representation in Figure 4.1 enables us to see how costs behave. We give the costs for additional children once the nursery class has been established for the first child. Table 4.3 shows the total cost, average total cost, average variable cost and marginal cost, as well as the average revenue and marginal revenue, for different numbers of children enrolled in the nursery class. Average variable cost is the staff cost plus the material cost divided by the number of children. As you can see from Table 4.3, at the fourteenth child and twenty-seventh child, there is a sharp increase in marginal costs as a staff member is added. After the additional teacher is employed, average variable costs increase and then decrease as the number of children rises. When a thirteenth child is added staffing policies in the school require that either a teaching assistant is employed (at 27 children) or the school will state that full capacity has been reached. Average total, average variable and marginal costs are also shown graphically in Figure 4.1.

The school needs to decide at what size the nursery class would bring in enough revenue to cover its costs. As can be seen from Figure 4.1,

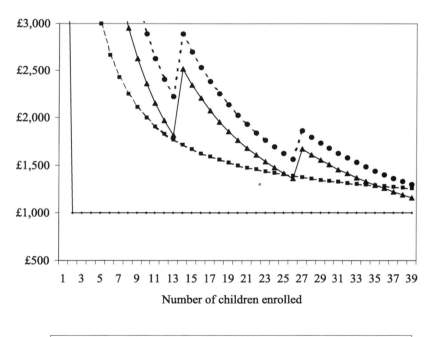

Number of children enrolled

Figure 4.1   Nursery class size: average and marginal costs and revenues

Table 4.3   The average and marginal costs and revenues of a nursery class

No. of children	Total cost	Average total cost	Average variable cost	Marginal cost	Average revenue	Marginal revenue
1	£28,857	£28,857	£23,593	£28,857	£10,500	£6,000
2	£28,862	£14,431	£11,799	£5	£6,000	£1,000
3	£28,867	£9,622	£7,868	£5	£4,333	£1,000
4	£28,872	£7,218	£5,902	£5	£3,500	£1,000
5	£28,877	£5,775	£4,723	£5	£3,000	£1,000
6	£28,882	£4,814	£3,936	£5	£2,667	£1,000
7	£28,887	£4,127	£3,375	£5	£2,429	£1,000
8	£28,892	£3,611	£2,953	£5	£2,250	£1,000
9	£28,897	£3,211	£2,626	£5	£2,111	£1,000
10	£28,902	£2,890	£2,364	£5	£2,000	£1,000
11	£28,907	£2,628	£2,149	£5	£1,909	£1,000
12	£28,912	£2,409	£1,971	£5	£1,833	£1,000
13	£28,917	£2,224	£1,819	£5	£1,769	£1,000
14	£40,493	£2,892	£2,516	£11,576	£1,714	£1,000
15	£40,498	£2,700	£2,349	£5	£1,667	£1,000
16	£40,503	£2,531	£2,202	£5	£1,625	£1,000
17	£40,508	£2,383	£2,073	£5	£1,588	£1,000
18	£40,513	£2,251	£1,958	£5	£1,556	£1,000
19	£40,518	£2,133	£1,855	£5	£1,526	£1,000
20	£40,523	£2,026	£1,763	£5	£1,500	£1,000
21	£40,528	£1,930	£1,679	£5	£1,476	£1,000
22	£40,533	£1,842	£1,603	£5	£1,455	£1,000
23	£40,538	£1,763	£1,534	£5	£1,435	£1,000
24	£40,543	£1,689	£1,470	£5	£1,417	£1,000
25	£40,548	£1,622	£1,411	£5	£1,400	£1,000
26	£40,553	£1,560	£1,357	£5	£1,385	£1,000
27	£50,279	£1,862	£1,667	£9,727	£1,370	£1,000

Table 4.3   The average and marginal costs and revenues of a nursery class

No. of children	Total cost	Average total cost	Average variable cost	Marginal cost	Average revenue	Marginal revenue
28	£50,284	£1,796	£1,608	£5	£1,357	£1,000
29	£50,289	£1,734	£1,553	£5	£1,345	£1,000
30	£50,294	£1,676	£1,501	£5	£1,333	£1,000
31	£50,299	£1,623	£1,453	£5	£1,323	£1,000
32	£50,304	£1,572	£1,408	£5	£1,313	£1,000
33	£50,309	£1,525	£1,365	£5	£1,303	£1,000
34	£50,314	£1,480	£1,325	£5	£1,294	£1,000
35	£50,319	£1,438	£1,287	£5	£1,286	£1,000
36	£50,324	£1,398	£1,252	£5	£1,278	£1,000
37	£50,329	£1,360	£1,218	£5	£1,270	£1,000
38	£50,334	£1,325	£1,186	£5	£1,263	£1,000
39	£50,339	£1,291	£1,156	£5	£1,256	£1,000

average variable costs are higher than average revenue until 26 children are recruited for the nursery class. But it is not financially worthwhile expanding the nursery class to more than 26 unless at least 35 children can be enrolled, after which average revenue exceeds average variable costs. From a financial point of view, the ideal number of children to enrol is 39. (In this example we have not used the standard condition for maximising profits, which is marginal revenue equals marginal cost, because the marginal cost function is discontinuous.)

However, it is not sensible for the school to consider only the financial rewards of running the nursery class since there will be other benefits to the school that must be taken into account. A nursery is likely to improve the number of applications for the main school and also to improve the educational attainment of the nursery children when they are older and in the main school.

Economies of scale

Economies of scale are another important cost concept in education. They occur when the average cost per student falls as school size increases, and in our example are shown as the nursery class expands in size. Small schools have higher average costs than larger schools. As schools get very large and need more complex and costly support systems, average costs rise, then diseconomies of scale set in. The minimum efficient size of a school is the smallest size (in terms of the number of students) at which average cost reaches a minimum. (Average costs of schools are not usually U-shaped, but flatten out and stay at a constant minimum over a range of pupil numbers.)

An important source of inefficiency in school systems is having too many small schools, especially after a period of demographic decline of the school age population. This occurs most frequently in rural areas where villages attach great social importance to the continuation of the local school, and it also occurs in inner cities as families with children move out to the suburbs. Reducing the number of schools will only reduce costs if the cost of transporting children to more distant schools does not exceed the cost savings of running larger schools and classes. Tao and Yuan (2005) examined the provision of schools in Taipei and showed the existence of economies of scale. However, when the external costs of commuting were added to the calculation, the average cost per pupil rose to the point of diseconomy and smaller, more local schools became economic. The policy of school rationalisation, which is a favoured term for closing and amalgamating schools to reduce average costs, is usually difficult to carry out as a result of the political opposition of those adversely affected.

In higher education the amalgamation of institutions to create larger ones has occurred steadily over time in many countries. Sav (2004) looked at the way in which economies of scale operate in higher education in the USA and concluded that there is greater motivation to achieve economies when the institution knows that it cannot be 'bailed out' from other public sources. This is one more example of how institutions are forced to respond to their environment.

The focus in this discussion has been on determining the types of costs, but it is also important to remember that resource allocation depends not only on costs but also on revenue. Schools and colleges that operate their own budgets have to work towards the point where total cost is matched by total revenue, from whatever sources that may be for the school or college – either from public revenue (as grants of some kind) or from private revenue (usually as fees). However, relating changes in activities, revenues and costs can be problematic because of difficulties in apportioning costs between activities.

Cost attribution

Sharing out indirect costs between the users of a facility is not an easy task to undertake. Generally speaking, as already mentioned, the convention is to apportion costs either according to the units (take the total costs and divide them by the number of students, or the number of classes, and then multiply the unit costs by the number of participants engaged in the activity being costed) or according to the area being used by the activity (take the total costs and divide them according to the percentage of area used as a part of the total area). In the nursery class example, indirect costs were apportioned to the nursery in relation to the proportion of the total space the nursery would occupy in the school. But it could just as well have been apportioned according to pupil numbers.

Whilst the concept of apportionment is easily understood, the practicalities of using it are often complex. It is possible to separate the direct and indirect costs of offering a course, but there are problems with both of these as the examples below show.

Direct costs

Teachers are not all on the same salary level, they do not have the same training needs or take the same whole-school paid responsibilities. As a result the teachers of one group may cost more than another. The issue here is whether to use the costs of the teachers engaged in the particular activity who may cost more than average (due to being more experienced and higher up the salary scale) or to cost all activities by the average teacher cost for the school or college.

The number of students it is possible to teach varies according to the pedagogy used. If a didactic lecture system is used, then it is possible for a lecture to be given to 400 students, but if a tutorial system is used with intensive lecturer–student contact, any group beyond 20 would be ineffective. Most higher education institutions use a combination of approaches and, as students follow different courses, precise apportionment requires making the calculation for each student and then aggregating it.

The practice in supplying materials of instruction varies greatly. Where students purchase their own texts these costs do not impinge on the college budget, but where the college provides apparatus, technological equipment and materials, the cost of the course increases markedly. Here, it is not the principle of apportionment that is problematic, it is the complexity of the procedure that requires detailed data.

Indirect costs

When room sizes vary, it is more difficult to attribute their heating, cleaning and service costs even though they may be used by similarly sized groups of students. Is it appropriate that some students cost more just because the classrooms they happen to have been allocated are more costly to run?

All students incur administration costs, but some groups may be more demanding of counselling, learning support or physical facilities than others in ways that are difficult to assess accurately.

Schools and colleges are usually supported by external agencies for teacher training, curriculum support and leadership advice. How can the costs of these be apportioned at pupil or class level? Whether these are indirect costs depends on which organisation is undertaking the costing of support.

Apportionment

The complexity of apportionment has been outlined by Simkins, who points out that 'differences in costs per student require attention to differences in the purposes of programmes, differences in the educational challenges posed by particular clienteles, and differences in scale which may give greater or fewer opportunities to obtain the benefits from economies of scale' (Simkins 2000: 173).

Per-student apportionment of costs is regarded as fair because the total costs are shared between all students, provided that costs are correctly attributed when some courses are more costly than others. However, apportioning per student costs by course can be contentious when some courses have much higher costs than others and these high costs are not covered by revenue per student. This is especially so, and potentially contentious, within higher and further education where scientists need access to laboratories and specialist equipment, and technical students require workshops, but the number of students and the value of their fees or state subsidies do not cover the costs of these courses.

Assessing value for money

As we saw in Chapter 2, cost is an essential element of efficiency. The relative efficiency of one school compared to another is determined by comparing their outputs relative to the costs of the resources used to produce those outputs.

We have already considered the concepts of efficiency and effectiveness in the early sections of this book. Levačić says:

> It is important to appreciate that efficiency is a normative concept. What ways of allocating resources is deemed efficient depends on what kind of output is being produced. To assess schools' efficiency in terms of students' progress in specific forms of learning is to make a value judgement. It is quite possible to produce output of little value to society but to produce it efficiently. It is also possible to be effective in producing output which is desired but to produce it inefficiently.
>
> (Levačić 2000: 15)

To solve this dilemma, the Audit Commission defined value for money as being 'achieved when the production process is both efficient and effective' (1984: 6).

While the definition may be stated with relative ease, the problems of determining efficiency and effectiveness recur throughout any assessment of resource allocation and use. You will recall that the variation in context, background and history affects every school or college. The point has been made frequently that educational inputs of any kind are not homogeneous in quality. However, judgements are made on the outputs of schools in ways that often appear to minimise these variations. Costs, particularly where they have been analysed according to the issues discussed in the last section, do yield some comparable data on the way in which resources are used and how different patterns of allocation produce differing outcomes.

When the revised national inspection system was being developed in the UK after the 1988 Education Act, the guidance to inspectors included the following:

> Value for money can only be judged after considering all the inspection evidence about the educational standards achieved and the quality of the education provided, setting this in relation to the school's context and income.
>
> (Ofsted 1995: 122)

Consideration of inspection reports led to the conclusion that 'most are an attempt to relate educational outcomes, after allowing for the social context to the monetary value of resources used' (Ofsted ibid.). Knowledge of costs is essential if such a judgement is to be made.

As the administration of education is increasingly delegated to local level, assessing the use of resources is increasingly made according to national reporting systems. National audit authorities have been instrumental in establishing both the content and process of such national comparative systems. The Audit Commission in the UK advises schools on 'Getting the best from your budget' (if you want to look at the full document, go to www.schools.audit-commission.gov.uk). Here is a brief summary:

The four best-value principles are that schools should:

- compare their performance with that of other schools;

- challenge whether their performance is high enough, and why and how it is functioning as it does;

- compete to secure economic, efficient and effective services from providers;

- consult to ensure that the views of stakeholders are being recognised.

The Audit Commission urges schools to use their resources according to strategic plans and in ways that meet both school and national needs. It also advocates careful consideration of alternative means of meeting the same objectives to ensure that resources are wisely purchased. It recommends that budget plans should be made to secure maximum efficiency and effectiveness. From a cost viewpoint, they also suggest that schools should have processes to challenge how resources are being used through forecasting, budgeting, purchasing and monitoring expenditure. All these require that the staff concerned understand the cost implications of resource decisions. To this end they urge that there should be a monitoring and evaluating system to ensure that spending decisions are carried out in the way that was intended and that connections are made between spending and outcomes.

Conclusion

This excursion into cost theory has been necessary in order to consider how available resources can be used to secure efficient and equitable educational opportunities for all students. This requires careful budget planning and preparation that examines educational objectives and considers the opportunity costs of alternative ways of achieving these objectives. Undertaking one course of action means giving up another. In the next chapters we shall consider the framework for this planning, with criteria and costs as our tools.

5 The allocation of resources within an educational organisation

In this chapter we will:

- discuss the importance of the budget;

- consider different management styles and their influence on budgeting, looking at rational, collegial, political and ambiguity models of management;

- examine rational approaches to budget planning, including objective, programme, zero-based and base-line approaches;

- outline a-rational approaches to budget planning, including subjective, input-based and incremental approaches;

- introduce concepts of strategic management, including emergent strategy and the relationship between strategy and rational planning.

Systems vary in the proportion and types of resources that are delegated to schools and colleges to manage via a budget, so this chapter is relevant to educational institutions that have at least some budgetary responsibility. Schools and colleges that manage their own budgets receive the majority of their revenues either as a grant from the state or a non-governmental organisation (NGO), or as fees collected from students and parents. Where schools and colleges are funded purely by grants, the amount may be insufficient for the needs of the organisation and they may need to raise additional sums either by fees or by fund-raising, including sponsorship, charging for the use of facilities or services, or seeking local donations. In this chapter we will examine the ways in which this allocation of funds is undertaken by those responsible, the involvement of the staff, the use of planning systems and the degree of match between plans and reality. The budget is at the core of this discussion.

The importance of the budget

So far the word 'budget' has been used with limited definition. In the general commercial sense, a budget is a plan that shows the amount and sources of income (revenue) and how it is to be spent. However, schools and colleges generally fall within the non-profit-making sector and tend to focus on plans for spending rather than on sources of income. Even those schools that are dependent upon fee income tend to work from the other starting point – they plan and estimate their needs for the coming year and then set a fee level by dividing the aggregate by the anticipated number of students.

With enhanced autonomy the budget assumes greater significance for managers and teachers in schools and colleges, because there is generally a clear recognition that there is no fund or group available to 'bail out' the profligate school or college. Setting the budget is an important part of the planning process as it is necessary to ensure that the budget is not overspent. Underspending, too, is a problem if it is caused by managers who fail to use the available resources to the benefit of students' learning.

Budgets are used in two ways: *forward-looking* for planning the future use of resources, and *backward-looking* when budget figures are recorded, reported and used to monitor actual income and expenditure flows so that management can be held accountable for how they have managed the budget.

It is important to realise that the commercial and non-commercial use of management terms can vary, and this includes the word 'budget'. The basic concept is the same, but in business there is more emphasis on revenue and profit. Non-commercial organisations, such as schools and colleges, may have to take the revenue side as given, but they should know about the funds that have been allocated for their use.

Anthony and Herzlinger (1989) see the budget as the core of both accounting and management procedures to ensure that all parts of the organisation are in balance with each other and also that each sub-unit within the organisation provides the necessary information to ensure well-informed decision-making. This balance is achieved by working at three levels. Strategic planning and control is concerned with setting and implementing the major aims of the organisation, for example, when the governing body or school council of a school decides to enhance the number of girls moving into higher education. Management planning and control is concerned with the way that plans are developed and implemented at the delivery level, and in our example could be concerned with securing additional staffing for science groups. At the operational level, more detailed decisions are made, such as sourcing the most durable equipment to allow for the additional groups to function. The budget should contribute to goal congruence for the sub-units, and provide the discipline of a financial framework and an annual rhythm for financial decision-making and evaluation. The budget provides a structure and links together the four stages of income generation, planning, implementing, and monitoring and evaluating expenditure at all three levels.

Handy (1993) stresses that the budget fulfils several strategic, long-term functions:

- planning to ensure future operations;
- controlling the way in which the financial resources are used;

- providing operational data for monitoring and evaluating outcomes;

- acting as a stimulant for change by highlighting the need for forward thinking.

In reviewing the importance and function of budgets, Handy (1993) outlines the Stedry studies which detail experiments that appear to show that there is a relationship between the importance attached to the budget by the members of an organisation and the level of organisational performance. Whatever the function of the budget, the appropriateness of the selected type of resource for the task in hand can be both a motivating force for teachers and affect learning outcomes. López (2006) has followed this through in a study of financial practice in the Spanish public universities. He found that although the units worked to annual budget procedures, they followed different accounting patterns. The result of this was that there was considerable variation in practice and inconsistencies in understanding the terms used. This is shown, for example, in the inclusion of the costs of part-time contract staff under the staffing heading in some departments and its exclusion in others. As a result, longer term planning of staffing levels was inhibited because the planners were talking of different staffing components. If departments are comparing budgets as a basis of future planning they should, he argues, be using comparable accounting structures.

It is quite possible for managers in organisations (and those working under them) to operate a budget so that it serves the purpose of control – which is important – but nevertheless to fail to manage the budget so that it secures an efficient allocation and use of resources. Hence, how the budget is planned so that it delivers efficient resource use is fundamental to effective budgeting. The official advice in England has the following rationale for budget use.

The benefits of setting a realistic budget

The benefits of setting a realistic budget that directs limited school resources in line with school priorities can be categorised as follows:

- Financial: a good budget lowers the risk of financial crisis in the year. Hence, the school is more likely to be able to fund its planned activities and less likely to spend valuable teaching and management time responding to funding shortages.

- Educational: the school needs to have the right resources to support the changing needs of the curriculum and the mix of pupils (for example, inclusion of special educational needs pupils). A good budget will allocate resources to these areas of need or development and therefore helps the school achieve its aims.

- Motivational: if a school is able to concentrate on its primary purpose (i.e. educating the children) rather than responding to financial problems that result from poor budget planning, the motivation of the pupils and staff is likely to be higher.

- Image: a school that is financially well managed is likely to have a better external image than a school with budgetary problems. Where there is competition for resources (pupils, staff, sponsorship, etc.) a school with a positive image may fare better.

(From: Audit Commission/DfES 2005: 2–3)

Management styles and their impact on budget-making

Organisations can be secretive about divulging the way in which they allocate financial resources. Bush (2003) argues that increasingly this is affecting the delivery of teaching and learning at classroom level as schools have been accorded more autonomy. He cites the local management of schools in the UK, the School Management Initiative in Hong Kong, and self-managing schools in Australia and New Zealand. He suggests that the predominating management style of the organisation will affect the philosophy and practice of resource allocation. By management style we mean the way in which the leaders – whether at institutional or departmental level – work with their colleagues to secure the best use of resources. Securing the best use of resources requires planning so that limited finances are both effectively and efficiently used. Where all the staff of a school or college think and work in a similar way, it is likely that the process of making a budget will be less disruptive and divisive than where there are marked differences of style. The styles shown by leaders at all levels include:

- Rational: where resources are allocated according to plans made at every level in the school or college – these plans are usually related to an agreed mission for the school, college or higher education department.

- Collegial: where the allocation is determined by discussion and consensus, and through the resolution of conflict between all parties.

- Political: where the allocation is dependent upon the strength and micro-political play of pressure groups.

- Ambiguous: where aspects of other styles may exist side by side and allocation is at best pragmatic and at worst chaotic.

A rational approach to decision-making involves three sequential steps:

- Determine the objectives of the organisation – there may be several and some of them may conflict (for example, maximising the school's exam results and being inclusive of all pupils), but there must be a single set of organisational preferences that decides on the trade-off between objectives.

- Find out about the alternative means for achieving the objectives and calculate the costs and benefits of each possible action.

- Select those actions that will maximise the achievement of the objectives from given resources.

No real organisation can operate a fully rational decision-making process, since all the alternatives and their relative costs and benefits cannot be known due to both cost and information processing constraints. Instead, as Simon (1964) pointed out, organisations 'satisfy': they do a limited amount of research and, on the basis of imperfect information, take decisions.

The above classification of management approaches, from rational to ambiguous, may be considered too simplistic. However, often a number of these styles operate within a single school as in the example below.

'Green Hedges' is a 350-student secondary school with an agricultural curriculum bias in the Cape Province, South Africa. The school is semi-autonomous and its total income is derived partly from government grant, and partly from fees and income from dairy and fruit produce. The principal retains 65 per cent of the income each year to pay for recurrent costs, such as staff salaries, building maintenance and examination costs, and holds a further 20 per cent to undertake 'major building work and to fund curriculum development projects' in accordance with the plans agreed by the school board of trustees. He then allocates the remaining 15 per cent to the grouped subject departments, using a formula based upon the number of students/lessons taught in each age group. This is calculated by multiplying the number of students by the number of lessons they take for each subject in each age group, with a weighting of 25 per cent above formula for the technological subjects and 15 per cent above formula for the science subjects. The agricultural unit has to be self-financing and is allowed to retain 60 per cent of the takings from sales for this purpose.

Within the grouped subject departments, there is varying practice. The staff of the English and Humanities group submit an annual plan 'starting from scratch and trying to meet all our needs'; the Maths department use a formula system based upon the age and examination level of the students; the technological subjects staff have agreed to work on the figures for the past year but to 'up them to cope with inflation', and the Science department, under the leadership of the biologist, 'fight an annual battle to get what we feel we need and reach some kind of consensus'. The actual sum of money allocated to each group of subjects is affected by the influence subject leaders have with the principal – three staff who have served for over 15 years each are alleged to 'have the ear of the boss'; in addition, the head of agriculture is said to secure additional funds because 'what they turn out is what the public see of the place'.

There have recently been complaints that, although there is a plan for curriculum development, the resources tend to be allocated to those subject areas linked to new technology and that money planned for new buildings is being used to purchase stocks for the farm.

In many parts of the world there is still little opportunity for financial planning of the sort outlined above – resources are limited, inflexible and uncertain. Even so, the most limited resources are likely to be used more effectively if educational leaders know what they would like to achieve. This involves making decisions about the best way of allocating the available resources. Plans should not be made for just the immediate future, but linked to a longer 'wish list' about where the school or college aims to develop. The following guidance links possible spending to the School Development Plan (SDP), a costed forecast of future development that forms the base of the annual budget as shown.

Summary of good practice

A school will have a financial plan or budget that covers the same period as the SDP. It reflects all the growth and development issues in the SDP and demonstrates that, in financial terms at least, it is sustainable. This three-year financial plan or budget will cover all financial issues, but in broader terms than is necessary for the annual budget (for example, categories of salary costs for teachers rather than a fully costed staffing plan). In terms of timing, the three-year budget should be prepared at the same time as, or slightly after, the SDP and updated as frequently as the SDP.

In terms of the annual budget, the school has to set this before the year starts (i.e. by 1 April for the financial year that starts on that date). However, because a key component of the budget (i.e. income from the Local Education Authority) is not known until the Local Authority sets its overall budget in March each year, the time available for detailed budget work is limited. Therefore, the first key to effective budget setting is to start the process early.

For most of the budget-setting process, whether annual or three-yearly, the figures used will be best estimates. A good

---

budget, therefore, is only possible if the estimates of likely income and required expenditure are realistic.

(From: Audit Commission/DfES 2005: 3)

Rational approaches to budgeting

A rational approach to budgeting requires creating direct links between the educational objectives of the school or college and the resources needed to achieve these objectives. The general term for this is 'objective budgeting' because budgets are structured around objectives. There are three main approaches to rational budgeting: programme budgeting, zero-based budgeting and base-line budgeting. Each is now considered in turn.

Programme budgeting

This is the most sophisticated of the three approaches listed above. Its focus is a programme: this might be a subject (for example, science) or a year group or a cross-curricular programme, such as health education. Programme budgeting is illustrated in the collaborative school management cycle outlined by Caldwell and Spinks (1988). Each programme of teaching is costed according to the inputs used to deliver it (for example, staff salaries, ancillary staff salaries, professional development, books and materials, equipment and other costs). The advantage of such a system is that the work of the school or college needs to be rethought each year so that adequate plans can be costed, reviewed, prioritised and implemented. The disadvantages are the amount of information that needs to be processed and the difficulties of attributing indirect costs to programmes.

Zero-based budgeting

This 'starts from scratch' every year with a blank slate. While not specifically programme-based, it does require those responsible for teaching activities to justify their intentions before spending plans are approved. One reaction to this is that sub-unit leaders inflate their requirements in the hope of securing a percentage of their request each year by playing the system. A further problem is that item-by-item costing is a time-consuming process. It does, however, ensure that intended expenditure can be judged against the objectives of the organisation or unit, and it is a useful approach during a period of change when philosophy and practice are having to be rethought.

Base-line budgeting

Base-line budgeting is a less extreme form of zero-based budgeting. The first step is to estimate all the costs that the school or college cannot avoid incurring in order to provide a basic level of education. This amount is then subtracted from the total budget revenue available. The remaining amount is 'discretionary' because it is the amount the school or college can choose to allocate between alternative expenditures. Careful judgements must be made as to which expenditures out of the total that can be afforded will ensure the best learning outcomes for students. This may involve choosing priorities between different groups of students.

A-rational approaches to budgeting

A-rational (not irrational) approaches to budgeting are those that do not pay attention to the objectives of the organisation, but focus entirely on inputs. The inputs – staff salaries, heating, building maintenance, stationery, books, computers, etc. – are the subjects of the budget.

Subjective budgeting

This is organised around the subjects of expenditure. Most school budgets are organised in this way as it is simpler to track and control expenditure on inputs than on programmes or objectives. Most computer school-accounting packages are set up for subjective budget coding. Programme budgeting also costs the inputs, but at the level of each programme. Subjective budgeting takes no account of programmes or educational objectives. The costs of each class of input for the whole school or college form a budget heading. The advantage of this approach is that costs are relatively easy to assess, in particular, as indirect costs do not have to be attributed to programmes. The disadvantage is that resourcing is not linked to educational programmes or objectives and therefore the efficiency of the budget cannot be gauged.

Input-based budgeting

Input-based budgeting is a form of subjective budgeting. It is frequently used when schools or colleges do not have delegated budgets but are funded directly by a central government ministry, district office or a local government unit, and their funding is based on the number of staff in post and the reimbursement of actual expenditure on utilities and other items. There may be rules determining class size, and hence the number of teachers for a given number of students, but frequently these regulations are not strictly applied. This could occur, for example, when following the rules would mean dismissing staff or closing small schools.

Input-based budgeting is still widely used. It was very common in communist, centrally planned systems and has persisted in many countries in transition, such as Bosnia and Herzegovina, many Russian provinces and Azerbaijan. In 2007 Bulgaria is finally reforming its input-based system of budget allocation to municipalities for running schools and replacing it with a per student allocation for both staff and non-staff inputs. Poland introduced such a system in 1994 for funding local authorities for primary education and then extended it a few years later to secondary education funding. However, many Polish local authorities still practise input-based budgeting with respect to schools.

Input-based budgeting does not provide any incentives to utilise resources more efficiently. There is no point in the budget revenue recipient – be it a school or municipality – economising on utilities or reducing staff when pupil–teacher ratios are inefficiently low, since it will lose funding because inputs have been reduced. In contrast, a per capita (per student) funding system does promote efficiency. If the budget holder spends less on one item they do not need, they can spend the money thus saved on items that are of greater priority. For the past 10 years or so the World Bank has been promoting the introduction of per capita funding in states in transition and developing countries. Per capita funding is a more rational system than input-based budgeting, but it is difficult to implement due to the pervasiveness of the political model of budgeting. Certain groups, in particular teacher unions and rural political parties, oppose any reduction in staffing or rationalisation of schools that would be the likely consequence of per capita funding.

Incremental budgeting

This is a further variant of input-based budgeting as it involves making annual adjustments to established patterns of expenditure by replicating one year's budget the following year, with only minor changes, such as the development of a new programme. Adjustments to reductions or increases in student numbers occur very gradually, leading over time to considerable inequalities in funding between areas and schools or colleges. As the bulk of the work of the school or college continues from year to year, the system has the attraction of stability, but minimises creativity in resource allocation and promotes inefficiency.

Bulgaria moves from input-based budgeting to per capita funding

When Bulgaria became a democratic state in the early 1990s it revived elected local governments. It has 264 municipalities of varying size that provide services, including administering education, for which they are funded by central government. At first, carrying on from communist times, this was an input-based budgeting system. As the population of school-age children declined, spending per student rose and the pupil–teacher ratio fell. The Ministry of Finance wished to encourage municipalities to improve internal efficiency by reducing the number of small schools and increasing average class size. But to provide municipalities with incentives, they had to introduce a per capita funding system. Initially this was done for non-staff expenditures, but in 2007 they introduced per student funding for salaries as well. Municipalities were placed in four groups according to the level of education, unit costs determined by size of population, density of population and mountainous terrain.

Table 5.1 **The four groups of municipalities and their per student funding**

Municipal group	Criteria	Funding per student
1	Population exceeds 50,000	800 leva
2	Population under 50,000	900 leva
3	Population per settlement less than 500	986 leva
4	Underdeveloped mountainous area	1100 leva

(Note: actual values refer to 2006.)

(From: Data provided by Ministry of Finance, Bulgaria)

Strategic management in schools and colleges

As already noted, rational decision-making is not possible in its pure form due to the unpredictability of the future and imperfect information. Therefore strategic management is advocated as the means to achieve a rational linkage between allocating resources and the educational objectives of the school or college in a world of uncertainty and incomplete information.

Strategic management is concerned with achieving a leadership vision in which resource management plays a fundamental part. Mintzberg and Quinn (1996: 7) provide a working definition of strategy: 'A strategy is the pattern or plan that integrates an organisation's major goals, policies, and action sequences into a cohesive whole.' Ansoff (1987) gives a more commercially oriented process view (by this we mean long-term consideration of the way in which the organisation functions in fulfilling its aims), but one which bears comparison with the world of education, including the establishment of yardsticks by which present and future performance can be measured. Writers in the field differ on the precise meaning of the terms 'strategic planning' and 'strategic management'. In his book *The Rise and Fall of Strategic Planning* (1994), Mintzberg is very critical of 'deliberative strategic planning', which involves drawing up detailed plans, based upon fixed assumptions about the future. He instead favours 'emergent strategy' which evolves as managers respond to varying circumstances, like yachtsmen, tacking and turning with the wind to get the boat to a desired destination. This requires managers to be relatively clear about essential goals, but to constantly adjust how these are achieved as they respond to changed opportunities and threats to the organisation.

Mintzberg argues that on balance it is essential to have some major framework for development, but that the longer the planning period, the greater the uncertainty that a plan will be achievable. When those responsible for school or college development seek a tight relationship between planned goals and financial management, they are likely to have to adjust, over time, both financial plans and detailed goals, while maintaining the organisation's overall vision.

Caldwell and Spinks (1992) see strategy at a local and more domestic level, although they recognise that the national context affects planning. Leaders, especially of the more autonomous organisations, have to understand the competitive position of the school or college and the major trends that affect development. They need to ensure that all stakeholders are aware of strategically important issues, and that evaluation and review are used to adjust plans so that they remain useful and are not negated by unforeseen events. Bailey and Johnson (1997) have considered the ways in which strategies develop in organisations and the implications for financial management. They distinguish the following approaches:

- a logical, rational and totally intended planning perspective: *financial plans are fully known;*

- a logical but incremental perspective which builds year by year on 'where we are now': *incremental financial plans*;

- a political perspective dependent upon the operation of internal and external pressures: *financial plans subject to power dynamics*;

- a cultural perspective in which planning is linked to the perpetuation of a set of shared values: *financial plans linked to status quo*;

- a visionary perspective in which organisational development is driven by a view of 'where we are going': *financial plans linked to the major objective*;

- a natural selection perspective in which future direction is determined by the strength of the competition between other perspectives: *financial planning is evolutionary but cannot be forecast.*

The process of strategic management usually involves:

- assessing the current position of the school or college related to its environment;

- assessing the current strengths and weaknesses in the use of human and financial resources in the organisation;

- reviewing the aims of the organisation and deciding whether these should be changed in the light of this strategic audit process;

- considering, and costing, the alternative ways in which the organisation could develop to meet its objectives;

- reaching decisions on the priorities for future planning;

- developing the longer term, medium term and action plans for the use of resources to meet aims.

Strategy and rational planning

Weindling (1997) outlines the differences between strategic planning, long-term planning and development planning. The way in which all these are undertaken varies because each school or college is a unique establishment. There may be long-term stability with inherent tendencies to incremental change rather than creative development. The leadership style may vary along a continuum from the collegial to the bureaucratic, and sometimes has no recognisable pattern at all. The way in which people work together, known as the culture of the unit, may be collaborative or individualistic. This may affect the structure of decision-making, which again can vary from the autocratic to the consensual. Scheerens (1997) brings these factors together and classifies the planning process as either *synoptic* planning characterised by high predictability or sequencing of actions, and *retroactive* planning characterised by reaction to events and incremental development.

The framework for strategic development may be clearly documented in some organisations, but in others strategic plans exist only as broad outlines that are little more than a guide to the future. For many schools and colleges, the process works in an emergent way in response to the changing pressures of the time. When strategic management is emergent, it will not be expressed in detailed paperwork and may never even get written down, even though the headteacher has a clear vision that is communicated verbally to staff and governors. Where plans are vague and emergent, it is difficult to tie financial management to them – the link is tenuous and unplanned or may be understood only by the headteacher. However, where the link between planning and resource use is made more explicit, financial resources can be used to optimum effect to achieve desired outcomes. It is argued that if the organisation knows where it is going, it will manage resources and structures in such a way that its aims and objectives can be fulfilled.

Although practice varies between schools and colleges, rational planning follows a common theme with a cyclic process of:

- audit – to establish the present situation;

- planning – to present and cost alternative answers for consideration;

- linking – matching component parts to the development plan;

- prioritising – establishing which plans are logistically and financially possible;

- implementing – putting the selected plans into operation;

- evaluating – measuring progress towards aims as a result of implemented plans, and then back to audit, and so on in cyclic fashion.

The rational perspective encourages an integrated, whole-school approach to development planning in which all units in the school put forward proposals within the framework of the strategic plan, and offer costed alternatives to achieve programme objectives. Effective development planning includes costed options and so paves the way for budget preparation. However, the interrelationship of plans and the eventual budget is not always as evident as it might appear in theory. The plans may not be the driving force that theorists envisage. This leads to the description of the link between ends (objectives) and means (resources) as either tight (often characterised by formality) or loose (usually pragmatic) or even ambiguous, even in the presence of a school development plan.

The tight model is characterised by:

- clear and unambiguous goals;

- a clear hierarchy of office and role, with responsibilities for parts of the plan assigned to named individuals;

- a substantial degree of centralised control;

- clear linking of budgetary decisions with wider planning;

- rigorous procedures for assessing decision options against the organisation's goals;

- effective and comprehensive vertical communication between levels for evaluation and review purposes.

By contrast, the loose model has a broader, more collegial view of management and is driven by its broader aims rather than tight plans. This leads to decision-making based on negotiation and consensus, and a flexible view of financial plans with frequent mid-term changes following widespread discussion and evaluation. In reality Glover *et al.* (1996) show that there is a continuum between the tight and loose approaches. Levačić in Bush *et al.* (1999) offers a typology of planning approaches based upon this distinction:

- embraced rationality: maintaining the fully planned approach;

- accommodated rationality: using plans as guides rather than blueprints;

- managed flexibility: as a pragmatic response to plans but reacting to prevailing conditions;

- value-based resistance: where leaders believe that they can attain objectives without the rigid planning advocated by higher authorities.

Edwards *et al.* (1999) investigated the extent to which the budget reflects the strategic planning within schools in an education authority in north-western England. Evidence was obtained by determining the extent to which schools were aware of, and used:

- Management control systems. Finding: there was limited internal auditing of the budget and even more limited intervention, except where schools were running into financial deficit or were offering poor value for money.

- Prioritisation of school objectives. Finding: school development plans varied greatly in their content and driving force and even more in the extent to which they were used to guide budgetary priorities.

- Costing of school objectives. Finding: there was a 'lack of any measurement criteria which enable an assessment of the relative effectiveness of applying resources' (Edwards *et al.* 1999: 319).

- The effect of temporal dislocation between financial and academic years. Finding: this clouded planning and inhibited monitoring while data were being collected.

They also found great variation in the extent to which the teaching staff were involved in the planning process. This led to misunderstanding of curriculum development and budgetary planning. Considering the evidence led Edwards *et al.* to propose a typology of school budgetary management as:

- safe hands managers – generally using incremental approaches to achieve an annual balanced budget with perhaps only 5–10 per cent of the annual budget linked to a planning exercise;

- active managers – financially stable schools making a move towards programme planning or zero-based planning for developmental plans closely linked to longer term strategies;

- crisis managers – generally in schools where there have been financial problems with budgets only balancing on paper and decision-making characterised by pragmatic short-termism.

Conclusion

Any school, college or department attempting to maximise the use of limited resources for educational benefits must have some idea of its aims and objectives, and the alternative ways in which these might be fulfilled. This rarely functions at one level only. Possibly in very small schools, a single senior manager develops plans to fulfil the objectives of the institution, prepares alternative plans and then takes the necessary decisions. In most schools or colleges senior managers are responsible for considering the needs of those areas of development for which they are responsible. They will, if collaborative and rational, seek the views of those working alongside in delivering teaching programmes. They will then submit their budget for inclusion in a budget at a higher level and gradually the overall budget for the organisation can be completed. This is essential if resources are to be used in an effective and efficient manner. In the next chapter we turn to the processes by which the budget plan can be completed.

6   Budget preparation

In this chapter we will:

- outline the process of annual budget preparation;

- explain the importance of estimating budget revenues accurately in order not to plan an overspent budget;

- consider budget revenue generation;

- explain the planning of budget expenditures and linking them with school development objectives;

- consider the wider involvement of stakeholders in budget planning.

The process of annual budget preparation

In this chapter we deal again with the second phase of the budget management cycle: the allocation of resources. We now look at the more detailed process of preparing the annual budget plan. This involves planning the next financial year's spending and ensuring that this can be financed so that the budget is not in deficit (i.e. spending exceeding budget income or revenue) or overspent (although this may be necessary if future funds are to be mortgaged for an immediate need such as unplanned expenditure on a new boiler for heating). The emphasis is on the detail required to complete the budget plan.

Whatever the size of the organisation, budgetary processes are very similar – it is the scale of the operation that differs. Computer technology is very helpful in computation or 'number crunching', but where facilities for this are limited, the same approaches can be used with pen, paper and a calculator.

Budget planning takes time and should not be left to the last few weeks of the old financial year. As discussed in Chapter 5, the budget is an essential means to making the school or college's strategic plan operational. The development plan will be the guide to setting the budget so that it is directed at achieving the main priorities for student learning. The development plan is usually set for three to five years, but is adjusted annually to respond to changes in budget revenues or the required activities of the school or college. Budget setting usually benefits from consulting with staff and other stakeholders ((all those concerned with a school or college). In educational organisations with delegated or devolved budgets, the governing council has some responsibility for the budget. In some systems, it is the council that is accountable for the financial management of the school or college. It is therefore responsible for approving the budget plan, advised by the school or college principal, who will draw up a draft plan for the council to consider and amend if it so chooses.

Budget planning involves considering both sides of the budget: the income and revenues on one side and expenditure plans on the other. As it is necessary to start planning the budget several months before the start of the new financial year, the draft plans have to be worked out on the basis of provisional estimates of budget income. This chapter first considers the income side of the budget and then moves on to examining how to plan expenditures. It is important that all budget preparation is based upon the most accurate figures possible. In both forecasting income and costing plans for purchase of resources, it is possible to make best-guess estimates, but the reality may be different because of a variety of factors, such as a change in the numbers of pupils enrolled or a sudden price inflation (a sudden jump in oil prices, for example). Finally, we consider the involvement of stakeholders in budget preparation.

There are several approaches to budget preparation. Official guidance in England suggests the routine outlined in the box below. We follow with a fuller discussion of aspects of this.

The full step-by-step process is:

Step 1: Estimate income – based on information on budget allocation from Local Education Authority, plus estimates for other government grants and income from letting the school premises and other income-raising or sponsorship.

Step 2: Estimate staff costs – based on the number of staff employed by the school and on salary costs, taking into account known retirements, resignations, responsibility allowances and new appointments, and including all social insurance contributions.

Step 3: Estimate operational expenditure – based on known cost trends for utilities, insurances, supplies, etc.

Step 4: Allocate curriculum budgets to departments or units within the school – use a transparent formula to allocate funds equitably in line with need and school priorities.

Step 5: Identify information and communications technology (ICT) developments – start with Priority 1 items from the ICT development plan. If funds allow, move on to Priority 2 items and so on.

Step 6: Identify premises developments – start with Priority 1 items from the premises development plan. If funds allow, move on to Priority 2 items and so on.

Step 7: Plan the allocation of any specific funds that must be used for particular purposes – where the items have not been picked up in steps 5 and 6 above.

Step 8: Verify planned levels of unspent balances – ensure the resulting annual surplus or deficit is in line with plans to either build up unspent balances to fund future development plans or recover from an overall deficit position.

(Adapted from: Audit Commission/DfES 2005: 4)

Budget revenues: income forecasting and income generation

One of the fundamental problems in strategic planning is that forward forecasting is a very inexact science. Some form of government grant funds most public educational provision and the context within which this operates is subject to change, according to local and national policies and financial well-being. Even if funding is guaranteed, forward planning of the budget is essential, to ensure that, at the least, the stated expenditure priorities for the year can be met. This is especially so if there are mid-term changes to the finances available, or if there is an inflationary situation that affects prices.

In a well-managed national public finance system, state-funded organisations will be notified of their provisional budget some weeks or months before the start of the new financial year and will find the actual and provisional budget very similar. When this does not occur, state-funded institutions have to plan budgets with considerably more uncertainty about their expected budget revenue and they will not be able to finalise their budget plans until well after the start of the financial year.

In systems that permit state-funded schools and colleges to carry forward budget surpluses and deficits into the next financial year, the final figure for the year of amounts to be carried over or clawed back is not known until after the accounts for the previous financial year have been closed down. In England, this is two months into the new financial year. Hence the main budget plan agreed for the beginning of the financial year may need some fine-tuning once the carry-forward figures have been confirmed.

Some schools in some countries, even in the public sector, rely heavily upon fee-paying students. Post-compulsory educational institutions are even more likely to depend on fees. Managers need to consider the extent to which fee increases will encourage or discourage applicants. In higher education, the elasticity of demand for places at universities and colleges is a factor that must be taken into account when students have to pay tuition fees. The World Bank has provided considerable evidence of the extent to which fee-paying in underdeveloped countries is financed – at enormous personal cost – by families who are faced with meeting the opportunity costs of supporting students at the basic, secondary and further education stages. The extent to which families will continue to pay for education if fees rise depends, in part, on the opportunity cost to the family of the child's forgone earnings and also on their perception of the benefits of education. In economics, the response of demand to a change in price is known as the elasticity of demand.

For schools in the developed world, fees support the private sector. Increasingly, however, in both the developed and developing world parents are being asked to supplement what is deemed to be inadequate local funding in the public sector. In the UK, considerable local sponsorship, matched by the government on a pound-for-pound basis, has been used to foster educational development. In China, many agricultural and industrial schools supplement inadequate grant or fee income by offering goods and services to the community. In the following box we outline the way in which one college has developed an entrepreneurial approach.

Banja Luka Catering and Tourism Vocational School

This school in the Republika Srpksa part of Bosnia and Herzegovina has 1,300 students between the ages of 15 and 19. It provides three- and four-year courses in catering, restaurant service work and tourism. It employs 68 teachers and seven non-teaching staff. The staff are paid by the Ministry of Education and non-staff funding comes from the municipality. Non-staff funding from the municipality is very tight. For many years the school has supplemented its income by running a restaurant that is open to the public. The students work and train in the restaurant, which also employs extra professional staff. It is an important source of additional income. Recently the restaurant was severely damaged by fire, but is now accommodated in a brand-new 520-seat building, suitable for wedding receptions. The bursar said, 'During the war people laughed at me for continuing to pay the insurance.' As this illustrates, making decisions about respect risk is also an important part of resource management.

Anderson (2000) charts the growth of entrepreneurialism in education through supplementary top-up fees, fund-raising and sponsorship. The greater the degree of entrepreneurialism, the greater the likely pressure from the stakeholders. Chiba (2000) has shown that this is an increasing factor in the development of Japanese education. He outlines the way in which additional activities such as 'cramming' for high schools, instrumental music classes and art schools are dependent for survival on their responsiveness to those willing to pay for such activities. As a result, there are problems in maintaining equity and budgets are increasingly driven by the need to sustain student recruitment. The effectiveness of the budget as the management tool for the organisation is thus distorted in public sector schools when fundamental values are compromised.

An alternative to generating additional revenue is to release existing income for spending on new developments by improved resource management. There are many ways in which this can be done. One is through the avoidance of waste. In European countries there is a tendency to use a great deal of photocopied material without assessing the educational benefits that accrue. Many schools in the Indian sub-continent have only one telephone and, although this inhibits capricious use of the phone, it has hidden costs in that people are frustrated by having to wait for the facility, or by the time it takes to fetch someone to respond, often at a cost in teaching time. For example, Glover *et al.* (1998) showed that staff with responsibility for organising subjects in secondary schools spend an average of 11 minutes per day photocopying, and up to 22 minutes doing administrative tasks that could be undertaken by an ancillary member of staff at one-third of the salary level.

Another way is by abandoning conventional practices that inhibit creative resource development. One example of this is the view that there should always be one teacher to 30 pupils in a primary school. It is suggested that a growth in class size to 40 could be sustained if there was a classroom assistant available to work under the direction of the teacher; at times the working groups in the larger class could consist of 20 pupils. Another fixed idea in some countries is that primary children cannot be taught in mixed age/grade classes. This leads to very small primary classes in rural areas. Multi-grade teaching can be successfully accomplished without a reduction in pupils' learning if the curriculum is adjusted for multi-grade teachers, teachers are trained in multi-grade teaching methods and there is more investment in learning materials.

Many poorer countries in Eastern Europe, Asian and Africa have multi-shift schools: two or even three cohorts of students use the same facilities during the day and evening. This makes for efficient use of buildings and therefore saves significantly on capital costs.

Multi-grade teaching

In a review of multi-grade teaching in the Commonwealth, Little (2004) suggests that it is the only way in which access can be offered to pupils in remote and thinly populated areas. It is also found in small schools in more heavily populated areas where the intake per year is too small to allow for one teacher per class. The range of multi-grade teaching within the Commonwealth varies from 21 per cent of primary schools in Northern Ireland to 84 per cent of primary education (for at least part of the day) in India to 91 per cent in Tuvalu.

While this is a necessity in resource use, Little argues that appropriate teacher education can overcome the problems that arise and, indeed, enhance the learning process in mixed class groups. She cites two examples.

In Sri Lanka, experimental work is underway to re-sequence the primary mathematics curriculum, so that similar topics (for example, shape, measurement, operations) are introduced by the teacher to different grade groups with differentiated learning activities. This work has been undertaken by teacher educators working with teachers. In the coming year, the entire Grade 1–5 Mathematics curriculum will be restructured and re-sequenced on an experimental basis (Little 2004: 12).

In Colombia, the *Escuela Nueva* Programme uses an integrated approach to improving teaching and learning in multi-grade schools in rural areas. Central to this approach was the development of learning guides and the introduction of a flexible promotion system, enabling students to progress at their own speed. In-service training and demonstration schools (which offer examples of good practice in curriculum and resource management) have supported teachers in their professional development.

Planning the expenditure side of the budget

Budget processes are continuous, although many teaching staff lose interest in the process once allocations have been made and the budget is put into effect in any one year. At any stage in the year, reviewing the use of resources in the previous year will be going on at the same time as the current budget is being implemented, and while the budget for the coming year is in the planning stage.

Knight (1997) recommends a four-stage approach to decision-making. This requires the planning group, however constituted, to agree a set of criteria against which decisions will be made. This could well be related to the aims of the school, possibly giving priority to basic education for all, rather than to computer technology provision for a few. These criteria are then weighted, for example, giving rather more significance to reading than writing strategies. The proposals under review are then graded against the criteria. The final stage is to adjust the grading in the light of comparative weighting. In this way, the potential need can be seen against the likely cost of each plan and decisions can be made accordingly. The budget can then be constructed with agreement on the priorities to be achieved.

Preparing the budget

Finding the right information for planning resource use is the core practice in budget preparation. Practice varies from country to country according to the degree of self-management that the schools have. Those countries with a high degree of centralisation delegate little of the budget to schools because staffing and building costs are determined by central or local administrations. Schools are left only to plan for materials of instruction within tight guidelines. In some countries schools are issued with textbooks, if these are provided, and have almost no money for any learning resources. All schools need to plan their expenditure to meet those aspects for which they are responsible and are therefore to be engaged in a budgetary process.

The budget format is also likely to vary greatly, although where there is either district or national audit control it is likely that there will be subjective and coded headings. This has the advantage of allowing comparison between schools (the basis of much 'benchmarking' data used to link outcomes with resource allocation). At its simplest, the subjective headings are usually:

- employees (teaching and non-teaching are differentiated);

- premises (with some differentiation between services, for example, water, and maintenance, for example, cleaning);

- supplies and services (often with subject-based and central administration defined);

- establishment (those centrally administered items needed to keep the school going);

- miscellaneous (a section that should be kept to a minimum?).

Establishing the base-line costs

Base-line budgeting is a practical approach, which is relatively simple to undertake, while focusing attention on how the school's educational objectives can be best met with the discretionary amount of spending available. Most schools have basic costs that have to be met year on year. These have to be entered into the budget at an early stage. The base-line costs include the provision of sufficient teaching spaces, of sufficient staff to ensure that all students can be taught in manageable groups, and the administration necessary for the organisation to function. A good starting point is the financial report for the past year or the current year. Last year's costs need to be adjusted in two ways – for price or wage changes (usually increases) and for changes in the *volume* of activity – that is, in student numbers and hence any change in the number of staff or changes in learning programmes (such as new courses or discontinuing courses).

Staffing costs are the largest element. In most school systems teachers are paid different salaries for fixed amounts of work, due to differences in experience, qualifications, grade, responsibilities or performance-related pay. Most salary scales have some progression so that a teacher's salary increases with their experience; there are often general annual increases in salary for all teachers to be included as well. Support staff will have their own salary scales with some of the similar factors that cause individuals' salaries to change from one year to the next. Before the basic budget for staff can be worked out, all these elements have to be added.

McAleese (2000) lists the problems arising where the budget year and the educational year start at different times of the year. This can lead to problems when the income for a financial year is used in two educational years, or when teaching salary increments are paid in accordance with the number of years of service, or when annual pay settlements bring additional payments halfway through the school year. In these cases the solution is quite easy: teachers' salaries are weighted in the first part of the financial year by the proportion of months in the financial year they are paid this salary, then the higher salary is added after the increment is awarded by the fraction of the financial year that teachers are paid the increased salary.

As well as unavoidable expenditure on staff salaries, the base-line part of the budget includes providing for all unavoidable expenditures, such as running the premises and renewing essential learning materials.

Planning the discretionary part of the budget: new developments

Once the base-line budget is worked out, it is subtracted from the estimated revenues; what is left is the discretionary part of the budget. This is what can be spent on the development work that is prioritised in the school development plan. To be included in the budget, development work needs to be costed. Table 6.1 shows a structure for costing part of a programme of literacy improvement in a primary school. The first column details the activity; the second, the resources needed; and the third, the cost of the necessary resources and suggestions for how this cost might be calculated.

Problems will arise in deciding whether to use the actual salary costs of the teachers involved or the average salary cost of all the teachers. There may also be variation in professional judgements of time and other resources needed. The above example also illustrates the difference between opportunity costs and off-budget costs. The opportunity cost of full-time employed staff (who are not paid extra for working on the activity in question because it is part of their job) is the lost benefits of what else they could have done with their time. This is not entered into a standard budget plan, which already includes the annual salary costs of these teachers. Hence these costs are referred to as 'off-budget' costs. These opportunity costs should be considered when deciding to undertake this development but should not appear on the budget as a separate item, unless the school is doing programme budgeting. However, if additional staff are employed for the activity (for example, a trainer for the school staff or a replacement teacher for the school's teachers while they are on a professional development activity), these costs are budget costs.

From each of the sections of the school development plan or programme, it is necessary to transfer the figures to a summary sheet on which the basic costs have already been entered. In Table 6.2 an example is given of programmes from a five-class primary school in southern Australia.

Table 6.1 Planning for curriculum activity

Raising standards and attainment in basic literacy	Real resources needed	Money cost: how would you find out what the money cost is?
Review literacy policy	Who? How much time?	Staff cost per hour Professional judgement
Review impact of interactive whole class teaching	Who? How?	Staff cost of evaluation Professional judgement
Intensive training for all staff involved in the school	Who will do this? Resources needed?	Consultant training cost Materials and software
Staff observation of specialist literacy teaching	How many lessons will need 'cover'?	Professional judgement costed at staff rate per hour
Develop an assessment process to track pupil progress	Time for all staff?	Staff cost multiplied by number of hours for development
Analyse school-based data and use to inform planning	Who?	How much time?
Evaluate classroom resources and their use: improve resources	What is needed?	Professional judgement as shown in review meetings
Software for pupil progress tracking or time for manual system	Cost? Training time?	Software Professional judgement and staff rate per hour
Monitor pupil progress and report: use for target setting after year one	Time needed?	Staff time multiplied by rate per hour

Table 6.2 Costing of programme activities for a primary school in southern Australia

Programme	Staffing days	Fee costs	Supplies and services	Additional administration
Basic literacy	25 additional to normal teaching	$A1,000	Books: $A4,000 ICT software: $A300	5 days per year for progress evaluation $A1,200
Health for pre-puberty course	5 days for small class organisation	–	Pamphlets: $A400	–
Special needs numeracy	50 days	–	Specialist ICT materials: $A300	–
Instrumental music	50 days	–	Hire of instruments: $A2,000	Support for rota arrangement 15 days per year: $A3,600
Library development	5 days	ICT for librarians: $A500	Book purchase: $A1,000 ICT: $A500	–
Totals from programmes	135 days at average cost of $A300 per day	$A1,500	$A8,500	$A4,800

The additional developments funded from the discretionary part of the budget can be entered in the budget plan in two ways. One is to break down the cost of the project or development into the various subjective budget headings, then add them to the corresponding budget heading code in the budget plan. The other is to create a separate budget code or cost centre for the development, for example, one named 'literacy improvement project', and record all expenditures on staff and other items to the project code.

The percentage of the budget allocated to the subjective headings provides some useful indicators of the way in which modification of the existing patterns or the development of new programmes will impact on the school budget overall. Similarly, externally imposed major curriculum changes, often following a change of government at national or local level, can impact upon the supplies and services element of the budget. Not all decisions can be made within the school.

Example of budget planning in Azerbaijan

In 2007 a pilot scheme of school-based financial management was initiated in Azerbaijan, in which schools were allocated a global budget determined by a formula that was based largely on the number of students. Until then schools had been resourced by rigid line-by-line calculation of budget elements that were determined centrally by staffing norms and past spending patterns. The guidance provided on budget preparation is given below and illustrates the need for budget approaches to be developed in accordance with the local culture.

Azerbaijan guidance

The budget plan should satisfy the following conditions:

- Spending can only be for the purposes of educating the school's students. It cannot be used for personal gain: this would be fraudulent or corrupt use.

- Planned expenditure cannot exceed budget revenue.

- Students must receive the teaching hours specified in the curriculum regulations.

- Staff must be paid the national pay rates for their grade.

- It is desirable that staff salaries in total, including social fund contributions, should be less than 90 per cent of the total budget, unless there is no possibility of spending less on salaries. More money than in previous years has been placed in the schools' budgets for non-staff expenditures. This is to enable schools to begin improving the quality of learning materials and the school environment and should not be spent on additional salaries.

Planning the budget: an overview

Here is a quick overview of how to plan a school budget, when it is allocated as a lump sum and the school decides how to distribute this lump sum between the various budget lines.

Step 1: The first step in planning the school budget is to determine how much is the school's total budget allocation for 2007.
This amount is given in the bottom line of your school budget statement. For example, Total budget revenue 59,000 manats.

Step 2: Work out your best estimate of the school's fixed expenditures.
Fixed expenditures are the expenditures that the school has to pay because it cannot avoid paying them. The fixed expenditures are the minimum amounts the school has to pay. Salaries are the largest item of fixed expenditure. You can change the total spent on salaries by changing the number of classes and therefore teachers' hours. Other examples of fixed expenditures are the minimum amounts the school has to pay for water, electricity and heating.

Step 3: Find out the difference between the total budget allocation and the total amount of fixed expenditure.

To do this, subtract fixed expenditure from the total budget allocation. This difference is discretionary expenditure. It is called discretionary expenditure because the school director and School Council can choose how to spend this money for educating the school's students.

In deciding how best to spend the discretionary part of the school budget, the school director and School Council are guided by their strategic plan for the school.

The school's strategic plan

It is recommended that the strategic plan contains objectives relating to three important areas, which are shown in Table 6.3.

When the school has identified an objective for student learning, it then decides what types of resources are needed to achieve this objective. The cost of these resources must then be identified. These costs then enter the school's budget plan.

Table 6.3   Linking the objectives in the school strategic plan with planned expenditures in the budget

Objectives in plan	Types of resources needed	Expenditure on resources
Student learning: Improve mathematics attainment at grade 4	Teachers' guidebooks Teachers' training course Mathematics equipment	40 manats 200 manats 100 manats
Student welfare: Set up a chess club	10 chess sets	100 manats
School environment	Renovate toilets	1000 manats

The use of spreadsheets in budget preparation

Spreadsheets are usually associated with the use of computer technology because of the in-built capacity of software programs

123

to make calculations as additional items are entered into the detail. Knight defines this as 'a computerised combination of a very large piece of paper and a multifunction calculator. Its format is a grid of rows and columns' (1993: 104). Since this comment was made there has been considerable progress in software development, and many schools and colleges now work with the commercial packages designed for schools that relate pupil or student data to revenue and resources. Alternatively, standard spreadsheet software, like Excel, offers schools greater flexibility and the final decisions can then be imported or keyed into the school accounting program. However, the final decisions have to be made by organisational leaders rather than by the computer!

Whether a computerised or paper document is used for developing the budget plan, it is valuable if it:

- includes all income and expenditure estimates in a coherent and consistent way that can be used year on year and between institutions;

- encourages problem-solving by asking 'what if' questions;

- shows the impact of assumed changes on the budget balance of expenditure and income;

- allows a range of alternatives to be considered;

- saves in time (and therefore, money) due to ease of automatic repeating of calculations of cost with changes in the ingredients in financial planning.

There are, however, some disadvantages in the use of spreadsheets if they are predetermined and created externally, and the school's budget must fit into them:

- the software program may impose limitations, for example, of calculation or of document layout;

- there is a danger of oversimplification by making input figures 'fit' the structure;

- the design may be too rigid to allow for educational organisational change, for example, if an attempt is made to use both basic subjective and program costing.

None of these disadvantages are incurred if the school creates its own spreadsheet; all this requires is basic knowledge of Excel or Lotus or similar software. The alternative is to do the calculations by hand using a calculator, which is much more time consuming and more difficult to check for inaccuracies. That said, schools that are able to make use of spreadsheet technology usually produce a separate budget for each activity or cost centre and then aggregate these to provide an organisational budget.

There are many areas of the world where resources are so limited that there is no possibility of working except with traditional 'pen and paper' approaches. Usually even in these situations, manual or electronic calculators are available and people are very adept at using them.

The involvement of stakeholders in budget preparation

There is a strong argument that the quality of public services is improved when the clients of these services have a say in how the resources are used. The World Bank's *Development Report* (2004) advocates this with respect to poor communities. It is argued that participation by citizens improves transparency and accountability, thus reducing corruption, as well as ensuring that the preferences of the ultimate recipients of public services are taken into account.

Participatory school management in Cambodia

The Education Quality Improvement Project in Cambodia uses a participatory approach and performance management. The project covers 23 per cent of the primary school population. Local school communities identify their needs and make proposals for change and investment. Funds are delivered to schools by the Ministry of Education. District-based 'animators' advise the government on how to improve its education policies. There is lively dialogue at school, cluster and administrative levels on how to improve schools; unprecedented responsibility has been devolved to school and local administrators.

(Adapted from: World Bank 2002)

From the perspective of the managers of public sector organisations, wider participation by stakeholders can delay decision-making, especially when difficult decisions are needed. The difficulty of taking decisive action when different stakeholders are involved is illustrated in the case study below. Although it is an English case study from a school with a high degree of financial autonomy, the decision-making process is replicated wherever schools are responsible for the staffing element of their budget.

Case study 2: St. Michael's Primary School

St Michael's Primary School is a small village school in a rural community with 120 pupils aged 4–11, organised in five classes. The headteacher is allocated three days per week for administration, monitoring and evaluation throughout the school and the total staffing is 5.6 teachers. The first look at the budget figures for the financial year April 2003–4 was presented to the governors of the school in November 2002. In summary these were:

Teachers and supply teachers	£208,525
Support and administrative staff	£ 42,800
Maintenance	£ 16,828
Learning resources	£ 16,000
Administration and insurance	£ 12,700
Total planned expenditure	*£296,853*
Formula allocation	£257,035
Other grants	£ 27,773
Brought forward from 2002	£ 6,000
Total planned income	*£290,808*
Budgetary deficit	£ 6,045

The anticipated roll is dropping by eight pupils (£12,000 or so) in 2004–5 and the governors have to plan for this from September 2004.

The governors decided that the deficit, although not large, required structural change for future numbers and proposed that the staffing should be reduced to 4.6 teachers. This would anticipate the fall in numbers and allow for additional salary payments for existing staff, which, although allocated under a government performance management system, had not been paid (£8,000). It would also allow additional support staff for all four classes to be employed instead of the two classes supported at present. However, they decided to seek the views of all involved. The following list of alternative suggestions emerged from the discussions:

- Parents oppose any increase in class sizes and suggest local efforts to raise funds and to increase recruitment of students. They feel that the governors have acted too precipitately and that additional recruits will emerge as the school's reputation for small groups becomes more widely known.

- Teaching staff oppose so much administration time for the headteacher and feel that reorganisation would be unnecessarily drastic and educationally unsound, but they also fear redundancy.

- Support staff feel that too much money is being spent on cover for teachers when they were away on training courses and that greater willingness to take students with special learning needs would increase local support for the school.

- Community members feel that more use could be made of the school hall for community activities and suggest that there could be more effective use made of sports facilities at an economic price. They also point out that parents are fickle and may well withdraw their children if they thought that class sizes were going to rise.

In the event the governors listened to all suggestions and proceeded to cost the alternatives. They decided to reduce supplies and services and to accept the parents' offer of fund-raising for the coming year, but then to plan for a reduction in staff in the following year unless recruitment could be increased by ten students. To this end, they decided to investigate earlier admission of pupils (at age 3.5) for a nursery group and a range of 'marketing strategies' including local publicity, change of school name and improved relationships with the surrounding playgroup organisers.

One approach to planning that involves stakeholders is 'gap analysis' (Weindling 1997). This involves comparing where we are and where we want to be. Weindling considers the importance of the stakeholders in contributing to the long-term planning process to enhance their 'ownership' of policy and practice. This presupposes that the budgetary evaluation enables the 'gap' to be identified. In the following chapter we will look at some of the approaches to evaluation.

Conclusion

The case study brings together the issues surrounding budget preparation that have been considered in this chapter. The headteacher and the management group of teachers and governors had to plan in the knowledge that they might not be able to maintain pupil numbers and that the deficit could be larger than anticipated. Under those circumstances, remedial action could have led to cuts in staffing levels, with an inevitable effect on class sizes and a perceived loss of advantage by the parents. If they then identified that smaller classes operated in other schools, they could transfer their children with a further impact on pupils numbers and income for St Michael's. The governors agreed that long- and short-term plans could minimise the deficit, but no school can run for long in this way – eventually the debt has to be paid and the adverse impact on future development could be catastrophic.

We began this chapter by stressing the need for realistic estimates of both income and expenditure, and we end it by stressing the importance of offering provision that can maintain a balance between expenditure and income. Once an effective budget has been planned, the next step is to ensure its implementation. This is achieved through effective financial control and budget monitoring, which we examine in the next chapter.

7 Financial control and monitoring

In this chapter we will:

- outline the importance of financial control and budget monitoring;

- consider the procedures and processes for financial control;

- see how financial control can secure value for money;

- outline the procedures for financial reporting and budget monitoring;

- explain the purposes and processes of an audit.

The financial control framework

In previous chapters we have seen that the budget is a plan for expenditure and how it will be financed, which should be informed by the relationship between resource use and achieving the aims and objectives of the school or college. We now move to the next stage of the budget cycle: implementation. This requires proper financial control and monitoring of the budget at regular intervals through the year. These processes are essential, not only to ensure that the budget is neither over- nor underspent, but also that those who are responsible for managing the budget can be held accountable for its proper and efficient use. At a minimum, accountancy procedures and accountability processes must ensure probity (i.e. that the budget is not subject to ill-considered decisions or, at worst, fraudulent use). This requires a clear financial control framework as set out in *Getting the Best from Your Budget* guidance in England.

5.1 The financial management information provided to governors and staff meets their needs by being:

- Relevant

- Accurate

- Timely

- User friendly

5.2 The school provides the Local Education Authority with accurate and up-to-date information in accordance with the LEA's needs

5.3 The school complies with Consistent Financial Reporting requirements on a timely basis

5.4 The school has up-to-date, documented and approved financial regulations that are implemented consistently

5.5 The school has up-to-date, documented and approved detailed financial procedures that are tailored to the school's needs and implemented consistently in practice

5.6 The school maintains proper accounting records throughout the year

5.7 The governors and staff have evidence that there is effective control over:

- Financial management systems

- Income received

- Payroll

- Purchasing

- The banking system

- Petty cash holdings and payments

- Taxation system

- Voluntary funds

- The school's assets

(From: Audit Commission/DfES 2005: Section 5)

At the end of each financial year, when the final income and expenditure figures have been produced, there is an opportunity to see whether planning has been effective and whether the budget has been used as a management tool. The budget is a statement of intent, but over time it is possible that changes are made and that resource purchasing is not undertaken according to the plans. There can be a variety of reasons for this, including differences between the estimated and the actual price of resources, last-minute decisions to purchase items that have now become essential, response to external pressures (for example, from health and safety inspectors), and pragmatic responses to internal pressures (commonly called crisis management!). The reasons for changing a budget plan can all be valid. There is both a danger of too easily abandoning plans and failing to keep the budget balanced, on the one hand, and, on the other, sticking too rigidly to out-of-date plans because, as one headteacher commented, 'We must recognise the sanctity of the budget'. Holding to budget proposals in the light of changed circumstances can actually inhibit the overall aim of making the best use of a school's or college's resources for the benefit of students' learning. Flexibility is possible, and desirable, providing that there is openness and agreement between those who are responsible for resource management and that the decisions contribute to using the budget efficiently.

Financial control and monitoring

Does it matter that there is a gap between what was planned for a budget and the reality of the budget when it is implemented? Most management authorities consider that there will be some variation because the budget is essentially forecast at least a few months before implementation, and revenues and costs are subject meanwhile to change. Nevertheless, the difference between what is intended and what actually transpires should be investigated and explained. In this way mismanagement can be controlled and steps taken to try to make the budget a more realistic document to assist planning, implementation and review in future years. This is not just at one level. Anthony and Herzlinger (1989) suggest that there are differing levels of management planning and management control, as we saw in Chapter 5. Strategic planning and control is concerned with the goals of the organisation and the broad strategies for attaining them. Management planning or control puts these into practice at a middle level, while operational control applies to the day-to-day issues, routines and processes. Thinking back to budget preparation, the strategic level would be a stated objective, such as improving boys' attainment compared with that of girls; the management level would be concerned to develop departmental plans to meet these aims, and the operational level would be concerned with securing the resources through ordering, checking and adding goods to inventories.

In strategic terms there will be concerns whether the budget, as planned, has been effective in securing the aims and objectives of the school or college. This may be judged variously, but requires consideration of whether value for money, efficiency and effectiveness have been achieved through the resource use. In management terms the same questions are required of each of the major spending departments. The budget also exists at a functional level – operational control – to ensure that all the elements within the organisation work within an overall plan and do not make purchasing decisions at any level that would inhibit organisational effectiveness. At its simplest, and as part of operational control, there may be concerns that the financial resources have been misappropriated either by accident or design. If there is concern for the probity of the system, it may be that the system requires tightening.

There are two elements to financial control. Although the phrase 'monitoring and evaluation' is used fairly readily, it is important to distinguish between the two. Monitoring is a more limited activity than evaluation and involves checking that what was planned has actually occurred. Evaluation is a broader and more demanding activity that requires judgements to be made about the value of resource expenditure and of the activities to the organisation or other stakeholders. Evaluation of the budget is the subject of Chapter 8: here we concentrate on monitoring the budget.

Monitoring

This is undertaken through regular checks of the intended expenditure at a stage in the year under any subjective heading and the actual expenditure at that time. In order to monitor properly, it is first necessary to *profile* the budget. Profiling means entering commitments to spend in each month as they are likely to occur. Hence heating costs will be larger in winter than in summer, whereas the salary bill will be anticipated to be the same per month until the month when annual increments are due. Having undertaken a proper profile, it is possible to examine discrepancies between planned and actual expenditure (where the latter includes commitments to spend).

Where discrepancies occur they may be due to incorrect 'posting' of payments by wrongly entering data; a mismatch between order and payment so that the payment is posted to a later period or to the wrong budget code; a failure to order in accordance with the budget, and an overspend related to cost increases or purchasing greater quantities than planned. The answer to the question of mismatch is indicative of the need for tighter management of the budget. There is an increasing amount of supportive data that can help schools and colleges to understand fluctuation shown in monitoring. These include: the use of spreadsheets to date orders, amount, invoice total, and payment dates; monitoring cash collection and banking procedures; tracking the progress of budgetary intentions (for example, in staff advertising); noting over- and under-use of resources to overcome waste, and the use of unit costing for comparable outcomes (for example, does one examination pass in History cost more or less than one in Geography)?

The concept of economy can be relevant to financial monitoring and used as a management control because it is about making sure that the purchasing and use of resources is done at least cost, hopefully for given quality. Despite the best of intentions, this can go wrong.

Avoiding poor decisions

During the last ten years of the twentieth century many English schools became self-governing and were totally responsible for using the funds paid directly by the government. They are, however, regulated – via instruments of government, including those for finance. Inexperience and failure to follow proper procedures meant that some schools encountered problems because they did not understand commercial practice.

One such school had problems with a flat roof over its gymnasium. One of the governors spoke to a friend of his who had a small business repairing flat garage roofs and he agreed to undertake the work on the gymnasium. The problems, however,

---

were greater than had been anticipated, the scale of the operation was much larger than the contractor had envisaged, and the workers were unused to the techniques for such a large area of repair. In the event, the roof collapsed, leaving the school to find a much greater amount of money than had originally been set aside for the work and the budget for the coming three years was adversely affected.

(From: Bush *et al.* 1993)

Schools with good monitoring systems will ensure that orders for goods are only placed after the robustness of materials has been checked to ensure that no better quality could be obtained for the same price. There are problems where the curriculum is centralised to the extent that specified textbooks are required with no scope for competitive purchases, but many school materials can be subject to competitive tendering to ensure the best value for money. That said, there are opportunity costs involved – schools with purchasing committees sometimes spend long hours considering alternative suppliers and specifications for only minimal improvements in quality for price. Centralised purchasing systems or consortia of schools may overcome these problems because they:

- are more likely to have specialist knowledge of producers and products;

- are more likely to have the advantages of large-scale purchasing;

- can more readily pursue a cause when goods do not come up to expectations.

So far it is clear that economy is best achieved in the purchase of goods, but there are similar advantages in pursuing economy in purchasing services. In attempts to secure better value for money some countries require that services are put out to tender and then judged according to the specifications given in the tender document. School cleaning, catering and maintenance are typical examples, but enhanced entrepreneurialism has led to supply staff to cover for absent teachers and advisory services to be similarly organised.

Procedures and processes for financial control

As we have already said, financial control is essential to ensure that there is no mismanagement of resources. This requires probity, a combination of transparency and administrative practice that can track how and where resources have been used. Whatever the criteria for the relationship between resources and outcomes, there is a requirement that the funds are managed in the right way. Operational financial management is concerned with ensuring that money allocated in the budget is properly spent on authorised purchases. It also endeavours to monitor the implementation of spending plans according to the budget or, with good reason, as a deviation from the budget.

Financial control is shown in the following areas of administration:

- purchasing goods and contracting services;

- banking funds paid into and by the school or college;

- managing the payroll for all employees;

- security of assets;

- maintaining petty cash accounts;

137

- maintaining voluntary funds;

- insurance matters;

- increasingly, ensuring data security to prevent the misuse of information.

Although it is assumed in countries with overall low levels of corruption that all those involved in education are of the highest moral character, even in these countries financial mismanagement occurs on occasion in schools and colleges. This may not be a deliberate act but could be the result of a failure to check details, carelessness in putting money into the office or a bank, or the use of 'short cuts' that appear to be cheaper than the recommended purchasing procedure. It also arises from deliberate fraud by employees, usually the financial administrator or headteacher. Problems may also arise because of the complexity of the organisation. Knight (1993) points out that the growth of self-management has increased the opportunity for mismanagement through:

- enhanced opportunity for fraud because of the greater size of locally managed financial resources;

- minimising of audit controls in schools in order to lower the overhead costs of administration;

- decentralising of functions to cost centres makes separation of duties more difficult to achieve – in a one-person subject department, for example, the same person deals with ordering and receiving goods;

- local processing of orders and payments may not be noted by central controls, especially where administrators are under great pressure.

In a recent report on the opportunities for financial mismanagement in a developed country, auditors noted that goods were being ordered from 'friendly' suppliers who were then making a payment to the head; that students were paying bribes to teachers to ensure good marks for project work; that payments were being made to headteachers of schools that were perceived to be 'good' to ensure admission, and that school equipment was being hired out, or even sold off, once it had been delivered to the school (Penton Media 2007). Another potential problem area is that of petty cash, the fund from which minor payments are made to teaching and administrative staff. Guidance points to the need for a robust control system.

Petty cash

Sometimes it is simpler to make small purchases with petty cash. However, petty cash is a portable and attractive asset. In order to prevent the fraudulent use of petty cash, therefore, it is important that it is properly controlled. Fraud is not, however, the only risk associated with petty cash. The major potential risks associated with the use of petty cash are that:

- normal payment procedures may be bypassed

- duplicate payments may be made

- it is used for the cashing of personal cheques

- it may be stolen.

Key control should therefore be in place covering the:

- authorisation of the use of petty cash

- recording of petty cash transactions

• secure storage of petty cash.

As with other payments and transactions, those involving petty cash should be subject to the same principles of probity and accountability. One person should not be responsible for all aspects of administration of petty cash, such as authorisation of usage, making payments, reconciliation of the petty cash account, etc.

It is also important that the responsibilities and authorisation limits of those with delegated responsibility for the petty cash account are clear and known by all school staff.

(From: Audit Commission/DfES 2005: 6)

In order to overcome potential problems with all financial practices, auditors suggest five essential principles:

• There should be a separation of powers within the system. The same person should not place the order for goods, check their arrival and then arrange for payment. Neither should the same person collect and count cash and then be responsible for its banking or the reconciliation of the bank statement with the school account.

• Contracts with suppliers of goods and services should include full and rigorous specifications, require that tenders are submitted following open advertising and be subject to monitoring and final approval before payment.

• Payments should only be made by authorised signatories (often requiring two signatures for payments over a stated amount) and only on the presentation of authenticated delivery notes for the goods or services provided.

- All sections of the school or college should maintain complete inventories of all stock when goods arrive in the department, which should be available for independent checking at all times.

- There should be firm guidelines for financial practice within the school or college, including responsibilities, procedures and the necessary record-keeping for both official and unofficial funds.

Three illustrations from an auditors' report on a rural school illustrate the need for operational control so that 'real money' is properly used.

Auditors' report

At Bushbank High School, four science classrooms required re-wiring as a matter of some urgency. There had been several small fires as a result of these wiring problems and the headteacher sought permission for the work to go to competitive tender. There were no responses to the advertisement and so, given the need for speedy repairs, the headteacher asked a friend from his local social club to undertake the work. Some months later there was a major fire, caused by inadequate insulation of a junction box. The contractor then admitted that he had no insurance to cover such damage – and the headteacher found that the school was not covered for work undertaken by unqualified contractors.

All major work should be subject to quotations from three registered suppliers and only undertaken when a binding contract specifying responsibilities has been agreed.

The photocopier in the same school had been purchased by the community but was looked after by one of the secretarial staff. It was known in the neighbourhood that he was prepared to undertake copying for local people. After some time the

---

headteacher noticed that there were many more visitors to the office than the cash in the photocopying account suggested.

All photocopying work should be authorised by a senior manager, and recorded and balanced against receipts on a weekly basis.

Bushbank was well equipped for rural industrial training and had received a considerable amount of refurbished equipment from an international charity. Two years later a local officer from the charity noticed that there was once again a great need for hoes, forks and rakes. When questioned, the ancillary member of staff responded that the equipment had been inferior and that many items had been thrown away.

Disposal of all resources should be undertaken according to an agreed procedure and only after a senior manager has authorised, and recorded, disposal.

Securing value for money

While there are arguments that can be made for decentralisation, there are also concerns that the quality of resources may be so variable that productive efficiency is compromised. Financial control offers a mechanism for securing value for money. Despite all the efforts made by those responsible for financial administration, it is not always possible to ensure that resources are consistent in quality. Some educational organisations endeavour to overcome this. For physical resources this is usually through centralised purchasing schemes. These have the great advantage that the purchasing power of all schools combined is far greater than that of individual schools and so items are cheaper to buy. Usually the quality assurance requirements are more rigorously enforced through specialist purchasing officers, and competition between suppliers is such that they will strive to offer value for money for the same goods. Responsibility for purchasing, however, remains with the governing body or school council of the school. To this end many schools have a purchasing advisory committee that offers advice, and sometimes direction, to the staff responsible for securing resources in the school.

Some physical items cannot be centrally purchased because they are particular to the school or college. Though it is possible to have centrally arranged contracts for services for several schools, these often offer the individual school insufficient control of the specification of the service. Such services include building repairs, grounds maintenance and some aspects of catering provision. In order to ensure some consistency and to enable checking of purchasing, authorities usually require the use of contracts. These are advantageous in that:

- they specify exactly what is to be provided by way of service and outline the criteria by which successful completion can be judged;

- they are usually competitive in that several suppliers may be approached by the purchasing authority who will usually be bound to take the lowest tender for comparable service;

- they are usually supported by the technical experts from central administration – few schools can claim to have a plumbing specialist on their staff;

- they do provide some legal support if there is any attempt by contractors to renege on a contractual requirement.

Securing value for money in purchasing human resources is neither as objective nor as certain as that for physical resources; despite all efforts, human beings are variable in nature and capacity. Most national systems require that schools or colleges should ensure consistent quality in human resources, no matter the degree of devolution. To achieve this they are required to appoint only teaching staff who have followed a recognised and approved course of subject-specific and professional training. However, there is some variation in this – in those subject areas where there are national shortages, professional training can be minimised or undertaken during the initial teaching experience, or in a variation in acceptable professional training (for example, where any social service training is acceptable for special needs teaching).

The greater the degree of decentralisation, the more likely it is that there will be variation in the interpretation of national guidelines. This may lead to considerations of cost and some balance of these against potential effectiveness. Changes in the salary structures for England and Wales have led to allegations that schools are employing younger, less experienced teachers because they are less expensive than those who have considerable experience. The counter-argument is that schools should employ staff who offer a balance of age and experience to maintain a staffing profile that meets all the needs of the school as a community.

Financial reporting

In 1993, after agreement between the Department for Education and the Audit Commission for England and Wales, all schools were issued with guidance for financial probity called *Keeping your Balance*. This summarised the rationale and the processes for ensuring good practice; it was later developed into the *Getting the Best From Your Budget* materials. The authors argue:

> Regular monitoring of income and expenditure against the agreed budget is central to effective financial management. It allows the governors, the headteacher and the staff to maintain financial control by reviewing the current position and taking any remedial action necessary. But budgets are not set in stone. The original budget may need regular updating, following consultation with governors, to take account of in-year developments. If this is done it is important

> to retain a copy of the original budget to support future budget construction.
>
> (Audit Commission 1993: 8)

In this way it is possible to regard the budget as a control so that probity is assured but there are opportunities for some change of action – provided it is argued, documented and approved by the school or college governance.

Reporting systems

For financial control to be effective in supporting the budget, it is essential that all the data are accurately and understandably presented. Usually this means that the accounts must reflect the detail of the budget, for example, in differentiating between money allocated to teaching as opposed to administrative or support staff. This requires financial statements with codes for budget heads for different sources of income, and expenditure on different kinds of inputs. It can be assumed, therefore, that the practice within a school or college will not change markedly from reporting period to reporting period. It could be assumed that the finance spent on building maintenance covers the same sorts of expenditure whether the report is for April or June in any one year. But consistency of practice within one organisation has limitations if other organisations follow similar but not strictly comparable practices.

To overcome this, most district authorities have given standard guidelines defining the structure of budgets and the codes linked to budget headings. This involves agreeing to use a standard set of codes linked to budget headings that can be defined (for example, in English universities casual staff are recorded as Y25). While this allows local consistency, there is still a need for a greater degree of consistent reporting to allow comparisons at the national level.

This has led to the development of national reporting systems based upon consistent practice. A Consistent Financial Reporting system was introduced in England in 2003–4. This software uses coded headings for all income and expenditure, and gives full guidance to posting detail to headings. There may still be some differences of interpretation, for example, in entering temporary staff expenditure on examination invigilation as an exam cost in one school and as supply staff in another, but the overall consistency in reporting offers advantages and goes beyond monitoring to evaluation. We will go on to outline benchmarking in Chapter 8.

> 'Consistent Financial Reporting (CFR) standardises, simplifies and streamlines the reporting of all school finances in England. The CFR data has been used to populate a website with a bank of benchmarked data, giving all maintained schools the opportunity to compare their incomes and expenditures with those of similar schools…CFR increases the level of accountability of school managers whilst prompting schools to become more self-managing. The ideology that each school is in the position to make the best decisions about allocating resources is at the core of CFR. Access to benchmarked data will allow school managers to make better-informed decisions when deciding annual budgets, thus improving overall efficiency year on year. CFR will facilitate networking between schools and encourage "learning by looking": less efficient schools will be expected to look to more successful schools for advice on best practice.'
>
> (From: Statement by DfES Value for Money Unit 2004)

Example of financial report for monitoring the budget by governors

It is important that the school's financial administrator prepares a regular monthly financial report for both the headteacher and the governors so that they can monitor the state of the budget and, if necessary, make decisions to keep the budget on track. An example of a financial report is shown in Table 7.1. The code and budget heading are shown in the first two columns. The next column gives the amount that was planned to be spent under each budget heading. The next column shows how much is committed to be spent, and the fifth column gives the actual amount spent to date. The school is now into the tenth month of the financial year. The expected total column shows committed plus actual expenditure. The key column to watch is the balance column: this is the difference between planned spending and the expected total. If the balance is positive, the budget head is underspent and if it is negative, it is overspent.

The governors seek explanations for both over- and underspending. For example, E02, Supply teaching staff for covering teachers who are ill, on courses or doing out-of-class work, is overspent by £2,643. But they are told that this is offset by E26, Agency supply staff being underspent by £4,690. This is because the headteacher has managed to use more supply teachers from the local authority or from direct contact and has not needed to make much use of more expensive agency staff. E05, Administrative staff, is overspent because of overtime worked as a result of additional work preparing for an inspection. E13, Grounds maintenance, is overspent because the contract came to more than had been anticipated, but E16, Energy, is underspent because costs did not rise as much as anticipated when the budget was planned. The governors are pleased that the overall budget is in balance at over £14,000, of which £8,000 is due to the remaining amount of contingency (the sum put aside in the budget to meet unexpected expenses).

Table 7.1 Beach Primary School financial report: January 2007 (tenth month)

Code	Budget heading	Budget plan	Commitment	Actual	Expected total	Balance
E01	Teaching staff	24,7443	57,000	18,9905	24,6905	538
E02	Supply teaching staff	9,000	4,264	7,379	1,1643	−2,643
E03	Education support staff	8,3740	21,670	6,3976	85,646	−1,906
E04	Premises staff	22,648	4,517	14,444	18,961	3,687
E05	Admin and clerical staff	32,592	8,616	2,5298	33,914	−1,322
E07	Cost of other staff	7,500	2,000	5,863	7,863	−363
Total staff costs		402,923	98,067	306,864	404,931	−2,008
E08	Indirect employee expenses	2,360	0	288	288	2,072
E09	Staff development	1,150	310	1,362	1,672	−522
E10	Supply teacher insurance	2,518	0	2,854	2,854	−336
E11	Staff related insurance	0	150	0	150	−150

Total other staff costs		6,028	460	4,504	4,964	1,064
E12	Building maintenance	3,127	87	2,618	2,705	422
E13	Grounds maintenance	1,374	344	2,611	2,954	-1580
E14	Cleaning and caretaking	2,172	165	1,682	1,848	324
E15	Water and sewerage	2,455	1,500	1,269	2,769	-314
E16	Energy	9,089	4,000	3,606	7,606	1483
E17	Local property tax	5,564	0	5,564	5,564	0
E18	Other occupation costs	1,670	0	1,149	1,149	521
Total occupancy costs		25,451	6,096	18,500	24,595	856
E19.LR	Learning resources	5,507	2,525	4,411	6,937	-1430
E19.FS	Foundation stage	2,000	194	1,793	1,986	14
E19.S	Special educational needs	0	38	25	63	-63
E19.GT	Golden time	300	0	26	26	274

Code	Budget heading	Budget plan	Commitment	Actual	Expected total	Balance
E19ICT	ICT consumables	5,000	4,000	887	4,887	113
E19KS1	Key Stage 1	2,000	33	1,560	1,593	407
E19OUT	Outdoor areas	0	0	500	500	-500
E19 School total		14,807	6,790	9,202	15,993	-1,186
E20	ICT learning resources	1,000	951	-451	500	500
E22	Administrative supplies	5,234	119	3,159	3,278	1,956
E23	Other insurance premiums	4,739	0	4,739	4,739	0
E25	Catering supplies	7,000	3,120	3,560	6,680	320
E26	Agency supply staff	5,000	0	310	310	4,690
E27	Professional services	38,936	2,322	36,537	38,860	76
Total	Other costs	61,909	6,513	47,854	54,367	7,542
	Contingency	15,000	2,000	4,850	6,850	8,150
	TOTAL ALL COSTS	526,118	119,926	391,774	511,700	14,418

Audit systems in education

If financial probity is to be maintained, it is essential that audit processes are put in place to ensure that there are no opportunities for corrupt or careless practice to inhibit resource use. To this end, most countries have some form of audit service and/or procedures.

The dictionary definition of audit is 'an official examination of the books of account'. This official verification is obviously necessary in order to protect those whose funds are entrusted to another person or group of persons. Such a restricted interpretation, however, would consign the importance of an audit to that of ensuring that the figures presented in a set of accounts give a 'true and fair' view of the health of the organisation, and that they comply with statutory requirements and accounting policies. The fact that very large sums from the public purse are entrusted to a variety of public sector bodies gave rise to the concept of 'public accountability', the development of internal audits, a consideration of not only the legality of expenditure but also of value for money, and closer scrutiny of financial procedures and processes to ensure that they comply with regulations and good practice.

Internal audits occur when a specialist member of the organisation, usually looking at the detail of operational management, undertakes this checking. External auditing is undertaken by employees of an organisation external to and independent of the organisation being audited (for example, the education authority with respect to a school, a higher education quality assurance agency with respect to a university). External auditing tends to be more wide-ranging than internal auditing, which tends to be confined to financial probity concerns. It includes within its remit, for example, the way in which the organisation is achieving its stated aims and making use of the resources allocated to it. Often external auditing informs and then prompts policy development.

Much of our comment on financial management is related to developed countries where audit services have evolved as a necessary part of public service. Tooley and Dixon (2005) looked at the systems operating for private unaided schools serving low-income families in Hyderabad, India. They found that a basic Supreme Court ruling that these schools should be genuinely non-profit-making was frequently ignored and that of the four other financial management regulations, only two were met in any one school. The authors reported widespread neglect of regulations and corrupt practice. They suggested that there should be more external auditors and that internal auditing should be achieved through a more transparent system of accountability to parents rather than boards of trustees.

The systems-based approach to internal review has proved to be the most effective method of arranging audit coverage. It involves identifying systems within an organisation and checking that they operate as specified. This is achieved by:

- documenting systems, perhaps by the use of flow charts, to ensure that all involved know how the system works;

- evaluating systems to ensure that they operate in reality;

- testing controls by tracking orders, payments and transactions against all records;

- making conclusions about the effectiveness of the systems in ensuring probity;

- reporting and making recommendations where necessary, and on subsequent visits;

- checking that recommendations have been implemented.

In a review of corruption in education in developing countries, Harber and Davies (1998) point to the fact that financial mismanagement may occur not so much because of planned malpractice but rather from opportunism. This can be seen in:

> theft (e.g. retaining for personal use cash collected for school dinners, trips, etc.); false claims (for example for travel which did not take place, for unworked or unjustified overtime, etc.); unauthorised purchase of items of equipment for personal use; improper use of petty cash for personal purposes; failing to charge for goods or services provided for friends/family (e.g. school uniforms, lettings, etc.); processing false invoices to a non-existent supplier and pocketing the proceeds, and making false entries on the payroll by inventing a fictitious employee and arranging to be paid an additional salary.
>
> (Audit Commission/DfES 2005: 3)

The role of external auditors is not only to spot where malpractice might occur and be redressed, but also to ensure that systems accord with district or national good practice. In undertaking this work they make extensive use of data that can be compared with those of other comparable organisations.

Conclusion

We have stressed the importance of financial control as a defence against wasted or misused resources. Although there are occasional headline-grabbing examples of corrupt practice, by and large most audit reports are concerned with developing good practice and securing procedures for gaining value for money so that effective education can be provided within the resources available. But while we may have a vision of what constitutes effective education, there can be difficulties in assessing the extent to which this is provided in any given institution. It is necessary to go beyond the control and monitoring function to assessment at a higher level through the process of evaluation.

8   Evaluating the use of the budget

In this chapter we will:

- define and outline what is meant by evaluating the budget;

- outline the ways in which evaluative data can be collected;

- consider the process of benchmarking;

- offer a practical approach to cost-effectiveness and cost-benefit analysis;

- introduce methods for estimating efficiency at the system level.

Evaluating the budget

The relationship between the ends and the means of financial management is the key to resource use, and this is the theoretical basis of all school and college financial planning. Evaluation is the stage in the process of considering how resource use meets the organisation's overall objectives. It is much more strategic in its viewpoint as it is concerned not so much with detail as with the impact of the plans to which the resources have contributed. It also prompts thinking about the quality of the outcomes arising from resource use. Knight (1993) suggests that evaluation should be concerned with financial efficiency by:

- comparing the figures from the completed 'out-turn' statement (which is the monthly statement drawn up as payments are made under differing budgetary headings) to the start of year estimates;

- relating resource efficiency to expenditure on purchasing plans for the school;

- securing value for money in fulfilling financial plans;

- evaluating effectiveness relating overall resource use to outcomes.

This is an essential way of managing development because it shows how past resource policy has affected outcomes. This may not be as easy as it seems. Look at the dilemma faced by Sanjit Raanah, head of science in his state-provided school in India, in reporting on the use of his physics resources for the year 2003–4.

Report to the headteacher; school year 2003–4

Physics department: Allocation 46,000 rupees

At the beginning of the year our plans were to purchase as follows:

Laboratory equipment	28,000 rupees
Consumables used in the lessons	6,000 rupees
Stationery	2,000 rupees
Textbooks	10,000 rupees

This pattern of purchases had been developed using:

- one-quarter of the funding to enable us to start an International Baccalaureate (IB) group (fitting with whole-school plans);

- one-quarter of the funding to give additional support to pupils in the first year of the School Certificate course;

- half the funding for the replacement of existing worn stock.

Comment

During the first term there was a burst main in Physics Room 1 requiring 18,000 rupees of unplanned expenditure and so we reduced the laboratory equipment by 12,000 rupees, the consumables by 500 rupees, the stationery by 500 rupees, and the textbooks by 5,000 rupees.

In the second term there was a burglary and so the unspent laboratory equipment fund – then at 5,000 rupees – was used to purchase a replacement TV monitor.

By the third term we were still seeking a good, affordable textbook for the IB course, but as these were all proving too expensive, we decided to divert the funds to the purchase of books for the School Certificate course. All the changes were made with the approval of the Bursar and the head of curriculum studies.

Staffing supplement:

Allocation planned	18,000 rupees
Laboratory assistance	8,000 rupees
Additional teaching	10,000 rupees

This was intended solely to support the additional laboratory requirements for the IB course.

Comment

This budget plan was maintained throughout the year.

Outcomes

The department has maintained an 83 per cent pass rate at certificate level, slightly higher than for the same pupils in the other two sciences. The IB course has gained from the additional staff input and we have secured a 92 per cent successful completion of the first year of the course. The visiting examiner commented on the need for additional texts for effective teaching and these will have to be included in next year's plan.

When I reported to the head, she asked me to think about the need for contingency planning because it would enable us to fulfil more of the plans when things went wrong.

When I reported to the finance committee of the school governors, they asked me to explain how an increased resource grant could be used to increase the IB pass rate.

Unless organisations have no plans, some form of budget for the use of resources is essential. Where strategic planning is non-existent, short-termism (meeting immediate needs rather than fulfilling longer term plans) and micro-political activity are likely to predominate. The budget is a reflection of leadership style as well as the organisation's context and culture. Judging the effectiveness of the plan – the budget – in securing the optimum use of resources is a means of judging the effectiveness of an organisation. When unforeseen events occur, sticking inflexibly to the plans may sometimes help to realise the intended aims, but on other occasions they may not and revising budget plans would make realising the aims more likely. Making appropriate judgements about what adjustments are needed to budgets in such situations is part of good leadership. In order to accumulate evidence on which such judgements can be soundly based, schools and colleges need to have a system that ensures that the long-term effects of expenditure are monitored and evaluated as both are required for the most effective use of resources.

Maintaining the information

One of the cardinal rules of successful evaluation is that it needs to be planned in advance. Failure to do this will result in situations where the necessary data have not been collected. This has been seen in some local education authority evaluations of information and communications technology (ICT) introduced in England and Wales where outside, non-educational consultants were engaged to ascertain the impact of new technology upon teaching after the commencement of the project, often from a commercial rather than an educational viewpoint. The evaluators were then unable to secure sufficient base-line data showing what the situation was in classrooms before the new technologies were introduced. To secure effective evaluation, it is suggested that all expenditure programmes should also include a statement of the nature and process of evaluation. In higher education this could be as high as 15 per cent of the planned total cost of a project, but as the National College for School Leadership in England has demonstrated, this yields evaluation of projects that informs future policy developments.

As the year progresses within any school or college, a great deal of financial and outcome information is accumulated and has to be managed. In a small school this is possibly an easier task and details are maintained by the head or a designated secretary. In more complex organisations, this becomes much more difficult. Increasingly time is being saved through the use of information technology. This technology has the advantage of maintaining and updating records as soon as the detail is entered, but it also offers the opportunity for material gathered in one exercise (for example, pupil entry) to be used as the basis for another analysis (for example, as the context within which examination results are achieved). The use of spreadsheet programmes has already been mentioned and, where the necessary equipment is available, the process of budgetary planning, implementation and evaluation becomes much more straightforward.

Evaluating the budget is only possible if the inputs can be related to the outcomes of the system. In schools and colleges this means asking how well any long-term plans have been implemented through departmental resourcing, at what cost and with what effects. An example comes from the efforts made by the government in South Africa to secure a greater number of entrants to university education. They require that secondary schools should show how they intend to meet this objective. Typical programmes include one-to-one coaching for students at the post-matriculation stage. A school seeking to implement this may decide to coach pupils following mathematics courses because this is a particular area of weakness at the post-matriculation stage. The school will know how much is allowed for the support within the budget, and at the end of the year will know just how much they spent on salaries and materials for the support given. It will also know how effective the coaching has been by looking at the examination outcomes for the cohort supported in this way and be able to compare these with attainment in the pre-support period, then seeing what improvement (or otherwise) has resulted. While any improvement may not be attributable to the coaching alone, it does provide an indication of whether resources used in this way have met objectives at both school and national levels. The plan is thus evaluated.

Management Information Systems (MIS)

Management Information Systems (MIS) are a response by industry and commercial interests to evolve the necessary software to hold and manipulate the information required in any organisation but to develop it in a way that suits specific needs. We have already mentioned Consistent Financial Reporting in England as an example of financial control. Considering the ways in which external funding is being planned for China and India in the current decade (2001–11) shows that schools are hoping to develop their potential for information management as a key to the better management of their resources, alongside higher level objectives of basic education for all and the development of education for girls at all levels. The project is detailed on the internet at http://www.ginie.org/cstudies/indonesia/projectsasiapacific.htm.

This complex project may not be without its problems and Baines has shown that there are disadvantages in ICT use, especially where technological stability and basic ICT knowledge is questionable, but he argues that basic information systems can be developed without the technology inherent in many modern systems: 'new systems and facilities…can support the kind of information use that results in real change in educational practice and management' (Baines 2000: 210).

Evaluating the budget as a management tool

The ultimate responsibility for budget plans rests, in most devolved systems, with the trustees, governors or the school council for the organisation. They are responsible for setting the strategic direction of the budget, for seeking audit assurances that allocated resources have been spent according to plans, and for ascertaining whether the resource use has achieved the anticipated results. For them there are essential questions:

- What progress have we made towards our strategic objectives?

- What factors have inhibited this progress?

• What are the current favouring and inhibiting factors for future development?

The answer to these questions will establish the 'gap' between planned and actual resource use and will indicate the areas of future planning that need modifying or rethinking. This is important because it keeps the strategic aim at the forefront of debate and consequently drives future financial planning. Generally governors will have delegated defined powers to the headteacher to use the resources to put the agreed programme into effect. This delegation of responsibility is not, however, an abrogation and it is still the responsibility of the governors or council to ensure that the headteacher is using resources in a transparent and responsible way and reacting to a changing context. The headteacher effectively puts plans into place by delegating the resources appropriate to implementing their part of the plan to the various levels of leadership and management necessitated by the size and structure of the organisation. Most schools require the heads of subject or curriculum areas to reflect on their resource plans and expenditure at the end of each academic year. This is so that outcomes can be seen against resource use and also so that the planning for the coming budget year can be undertaken on the basis of secure data. Within this structure administrators will have some responsibilities for the use of resources. They may report directly to the programme leader or, in some institutions, to senior administrators, who then report to leadership groups, to show how the finance has actually been spent and evaluate its effect.

Benchmarking

To help with this process, much publicity has been given to the use of benchmarking, which is comparing an organisation's or unit's performance on various indicators with that of similar organisations, in particular with best practice if that can be identified. Benchmarking can be done within an organisation, for example, comparing departments, or between organisations, either the school or college as a whole or subject departments across universities, for example. Because of the difficulties in education in identifying the impact of spending on student outcomes, it is much easier to compare schools or colleges in terms of their costs.

Applied to the evaluation of educational expenditure, benchmarking involves recording the expenditure in various areas of educational practice of different organisations or units within an organisation and then using this as a mean against which the performance of individual schools and colleges can be measured. In this way it is possible for a school to consider how it stands in relation to other schools of similar size and context, for example, in the amount spent per pupil or the proportion of the budget spent on teachers, administrative staff, buildings, operations and other items. If the school or department's expenditure ratios are dissimilar to those of other similar schools or departments, the next step is to ask the questions of why and to what effect?

Schools in England are able to use the Schools' Financial Benchmarking site. Here all schools' financial data from the previous year are assembled. A school enters the site using a password and can ask for comparisons of costs per pupil for a wide range of inputs. In order to make a fair comparison, the school selects values for a range of indicators, such as school type, size, location, percentages of poor students and those from ethnic minorities. This is shown in the example below for the cost of teaching staff per pupil. The school is shown to have median costs and therefore it can be reassured that there is little need to review this level of spending, unless there are other reasons to do so. Benchmarking against averages must be used cautiously. Had the school found that its spending was relatively high, this would not mean that it should reduce its spending on teachers. Such a benchmarking result only suggests that the school looks more closely at its teaching costs and sees if there are justifiable reasons for these being relatively high. The process is outlined in Figure 8.1 below.

Figure 8.1   Benchmarking using the Schools' Financial Benchmarking site (DfES)

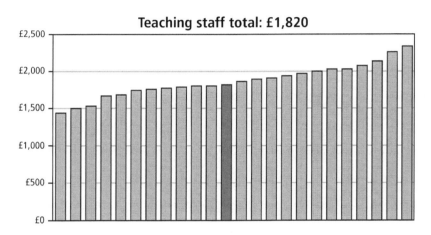

Comparative criteria

School type: primary school

Size: 80–140 pupils

Poverty indicator: 20–60 per cent of pupils eligible for free school meals

Ethnicity indicator: over 30 per cent from ethnic minorities

24 schools compared for teaching costs per pupil: the comparison school is shown in dark grey.

Cost-effectiveness analysis (CEA) and cost-benefit analysis (CBA)

Benchmarking, as in the examples given, usually focuses on either input (cost) and output measures. Cost-effective analysis (CEA) and cost-benefit analysis (CBA) focus on comparing inputs and outputs. Lay people often confuse these two techniques, but they are very distinct. Cost-effectiveness analysis only requires a physical measure of the outputs of the educational investment (for example, reading scores or examination results). Cost-benefit analysis requires a monetary measure of the benefits, which can be difficult to obtain without a lot of research. Both CEA and CBA take account of the time profile of the costs and the outputs or benefits. The method of doing this will be examined in the next chapter.

The essence of CEA is that it considers the comparative value of different programmes to secure the same outcomes (for example, enhanced mathematics scores). For example, if three different ways of teaching a set of maths skills are evaluated, the costs of each programme are compared to the progress made by similar groups of students on average in each maths programme. From this, the cost per maths gain can be calculated and the most cost-effective programme is the one with the highest maths score per dollar. CEA does not offer a means of comparing alternatives for differing outcomes (for example, comparing a programme for improved maths attainment with a programme for enhanced language skills since these cannot be measured in the same units).

If it was possible to estimate the amount that additional specific maths or language skills added to the students' future earnings, then it would be possible to undertake a cost-benefit analysis, as a CBA aims to evaluate programmes according to monetary measures of benefits. Since each alternative is assessed in terms of its monetary costs and the monetary values of its benefits, each alternative can be examined on its own merits to see if it is worthwhile. A plan can only be considered when it shows benefits greater than costs. The most acceptable plan is the one that offers the highest benefit-to-cost ratio, or the plan that offered stated benefits at lowest cost. The problem for much educational planning is that outcomes – other than examination success – are difficult to measure; it is even more difficult to give monetary value to educational outputs and outcomes to enable CBA calculations.

Here are two examples to illustrate what we mean.

Example 1

A large primary school was aware of pupil misbehaviour during the lunch-time break and sought a changed approach. The current arrangement meant that the headteacher was spending a considerable amount of time on pupil behaviour. An alternative arrangement was suggested whereby the number of midday supervisors would be increased and they would be given weekly training sessions on pupil behaviour. It was thought that this could save much of the headteacher's time. The result of the change was a 51 per cent drop in the number of pupils referred for bad behaviour at lunch-time.

Here there are two ways of achieving a given end (less bad behaviour by pupils at lunch-time). The cost of extra midday supervisors is their additional pay plus any National Insurance; the cost of the headteacher is his/her pay per hour multiplied by the number of hours a week that are no longer spent on pupil behaviour during the lunch-time break. To calculate the headteacher's hourly rate of pay, you need to divide the annual salary (with on-costs) by the number of hours worked per year – this can be difficult to assess, given that headteachers do not usually work set hours.

Cost-benefit analysis could not be used because the outcomes could not be expressed in monetary terms.

This was a post-budget effect of a policy change, rather than a driver at the planning stage. But the evidence would be used to decide whether to continue employing additional midday supervisors.

Example 2

A large secondary school offered additional revision courses during the Easter vacation for pupils in the year in which they will be taking public examinations. It needed to know whether this was an effective use of resources.

The public examination results for the cohort were examined and a linear regression statistical approach used to ascertain whether there was a link between attendance at the Easter revision classes and subsequent examination results. This showed that, after allowing for gender and prior attainment, there was a positive association between a student attending the revision sessions and their exam results.

The cost of the average improvement could be calculated from the costs of the revision course averaged between participants and compared with the average enhanced attainment for attenders when measured against the average for non-attenders.

The cost of the course had been programmed into costs for the year, and could have been subject to a cost-effectiveness analysis if alternative ways of securing improved results had been considered. However, a cost-benefit analysis could not be used because no monetary value could be attached to the improved results.

While the available evidence suggests that schools and colleges don't make much use of CBA and CEA, both examples show how comparing the costs of a change with educational outcomes within the school provides evidence that can be used to decide whether or not the practice is worth continuing. At the same time, it has to be remembered that education is a complex process.

Unless a carefully conducted experiment is carried out, with students randomly assigned to treatment and control groups, it is not possible to have a lot of confidence that any particular expenditure programme could be the sole cause of particular identified improvements. In the examples above it could well be that there were explanations for the improved outcomes other than the changed practice that was evaluated. In the primary school example, improved pupil behaviour might have been due to an apparently unrelated change, such as the inclusion of a human values programme in assemblies. In the case of the Easter revision classes, it could be that it was the highly motivated students who attended and it was their motivation, of which the school has no measure, that explained their higher exam results, even after allowing for gender and prior attainment.

Revisiting efficiency and effectiveness

These concepts, which were defined in Chapter 2, are part of the armoury of evaluation – but the terms can be misused. We revisit them here to stress their correct meaning when applied to schools and colleges.

Efficiency

Efficiency entails securing minimum cost for any given quality and quantity of service provided. How can a senior school science lesson aimed at a matriculation level be achieved at minimum cost? In educational thinking this appears rather negative, while the corollary of achieving maximum output for any given set of resource inputs is much more acceptable. Recall that the efficiency concept we are using here is that of *internal efficiency*; the social value of the output in question is not considered because it is so difficult to assess.

Efficiency is always a relative concept. In the example in the previous paragraph, reducing the cost of securing a given level of science attainment within a single school is compared with previous practice.

Overall school efficiency requires comparing two or more schools. If two schools have a similar percentage of students with above-average attainment in the national leaving examinations, but one is funded at 80 per cent of the funding level of the other, it is assumed to be more efficient. That may not always be the case, because although bald statistics tell us something about raw examination results, they tell us about educational quality – unless we know the students in the two schools are very similar in their prior attainment, gender and social background. Only if we compare the value-added results of the two schools to the costs of attaining those results can we determine whether one school is internally efficient compared to the other school.

Within a school or college, the unit costs of achieving specific examination results or qualifications can be calculated and compared for different lecturers of the same subject or even across different subjects and qualifications, to find out if the cost per qualification is recovered in the funding received for running the course. This approach was used by Jones (1987) in evaluating unit costs in a college of further education. Jones used a formula for the unit cost of an examination pass as:

Unit cost = <u>course length in weeks x hours taught per week</u>
        number of students registered for the course x pass rate

The factors affecting unit cost include the staff-to-student ratio and the average class size. An optimum organisational arrangement would be where the course population is the maximum number of students that acceptable educational practice allows, and where the teaching provided is for the fewest hours that standard educational practice recommends, and this results in achieving the target pass rate. This then gives:

Optimum unit cost =

optimum course length in weeks x optimum hours taught per week
Optimum population x target pass rate

Such a formula provides a basis of comparison between courses in one department in a college and similar courses in other departments as well as between similar courses in different colleges. If all that managers are interested in is what a qualification costs (because they wish to assess its financial viability in relation to the income the college receives for running the course), this is an appropriate approach. However, the relative efficiency of course provision in different colleges cannot be determined unless the students are of similar ability. If they are not, then the effect of differences in their ability on course results must be included in the assessment of student progress, so that the unit cost calculated is that for student progress rather than the qualification.

Effectiveness

Effectiveness is an even more subjective concept. It makes assumptions about the social values of the output, which are much more difficult to measure. The standard definition of effectiveness is the extent to which a programme or activity is achieving its established goals. This means that a programme of activity can be effective (doing the right things), but not doing so in an efficient way (doing things right). At this point evaluation becomes much more subjective and concerned with the organisation of teaching and learning, the appropriateness of pedagogic method, the nature of support for those with difficulties, and the context within which the school works. It is difficult to find measurable statistics for these and here subjective judgement enters into the reckoning. Educational reports looking at the effectiveness of schools often refer to good practice rather than to specific outcomes, and this is only rarely measurable. This is evident in the example below, which attempts to evaluate effectiveness in a remote, and unusual, college of further education.

A technical school in northern Norway provides sixth form technical education for about 300 students of post-16 age. Half of these students live up to 300 km away from the campus and some have never visited the college at all. They work through satellite schools in rural areas and extensive use of distance learning techniques and video-linking. One example of the efficiency and effectiveness debate arose from the assessment of students undertaking catering courses. Previously a member of staff had visited the satellite centres to assess work in progress but, following a training period, video-conferencing is now being used.

Efficiency has been demonstrated because the same output (the assessment of students) is now being undertaken for just over half the annual cost – teacher time is no longer spent in travelling. Whether effectiveness has changed is a matter of debate – the same number of students is being assessed but the incidental chats with staff in isolated centres, the ability to see what is going on 'off camera', and the opportunity for pre- and post-exam chats with the students has been lost.

More advanced evaluation techniques

Methods taken from operational research can be used to estimate the efficiency of schools and colleges. Data envelopment analysis (DEA) is one such way of determining how efficient a school is in its use of resources. As it requires a high degree of expertise and data from a good number of comparable organisations, DEA is not a technique for use by individual school and college managers.

DEA can be applied where schools produce multiple outputs and use multiple inputs. In simple terms, schools producing the same outputs and using the same combination of inputs can be compared for efficiency. The school that produces the most output for a given combination of inputs is deemed to be the most efficient. It is assumed that all schools using the same quantity and combination of inputs should be able to produce the same outputs as the most efficient school. The relative efficiency of other schools is measured in terms of the difference in each of their outputs compared to that of the most efficient school, which is referred to as the 'peer' school.

For each different combination of inputs (i.e. ratio in which the inputs are used) an efficient peer school is defined, and the outputs of other schools using the same combination of inputs are compared to the outputs of the peer school. Each peer school lies on what is called a 'technical efficiency frontier': no peer school can be said to be more efficient than any of the other peer schools. Salerno (2006) used this method to examine the costs of courses in higher education institutions in the Netherlands, and argues that DEA provides a more realistic estimate of costs than estimates built on traditional per student costing. This is because DEA calculates the cost of multiple outputs produced using multiple inputs, whereas traditional accountancy costing methods have to rely on attribution of costs using relatively arbitrary assumptions.

The Department for Education and Skills (DfES) in England has been active in developing information systems for promoting school efficiency. From 2002 a national database of value-added school performance and finance data has existed. The availability of these data enabled the DfES to commission a DEA analysis of secondary schools (Smith and Street 2006). This measured output as the value-added between the Key Stage 3 tests in maths, science and English (taken at age 13–14 in Year 9) and the General Certificate of Secondary School (GCSE) examination results taken by the same students two years later in Year 11. Four inputs were included: teachers; learning support staff and administrative staff per 1,000 pupils; expenditure on ICT, and learning resources as well as four characteristics of students (for example, percentage eligible for free school meals). The DEA analysis found that the average secondary school in 2004 had 94 per cent efficiency compared to the most efficient schools. The least efficient school had 75 per cent efficiency.

Education production functions

Education production function (EPF) analysis attempts to relate the output of schools or colleges (such as exam results) to the inputs used. It uses multivariate regression, which is a statistical process that considers all the variables that might affect an outcome and then estimates the size of the effects on the individual factors and combinations of factors that produces that outcome.

School output is related to the quantities of inputs used (such as teachers, non-teaching staff, materials, physical facilities) after allowing for other factors that affect pupils' examination results (such as their attainment before entering the school, gender, ethnicity) and school composition (such as the proportion of pupils from socially deprived families). Thus a value-added measure of school is used since it is essential to allow for factors that affect students' attainment, but are not factors directly under the control of the school, as are class size or expenditure on books. In order to assess a school's efficiency, such studies attempt to assess how far the resources used by the school have contributed to the progress of individual students when compared with their attainment level at entry or at an earlier stage in their educational careers. The average for all similar schools provides a benchmark from which positive or negative deviations can be measured. While many education production function studies have been completed, the findings are still much disputed among education economists because of the difficulties experienced in getting sufficiently good data to be able to estimate a causal effect of resources on school outputs. For example, a study by Jenkins *et al.* (2006) of English secondary schools found small statistically significant effects on GCSE results of expenditure per student and the pupil–teacher ratio.

Qualitative approaches to judging school efficiency

Because of the difficulty in obtaining quantitative measures of school efficiency, qualitative approaches are used when such judgements need to be made. In England the Office for Standards in Education Guidelines for inspecting schools (Ofsted) includes an assessment of 'how effectively and efficiently resources are deployed to achieve value for money'. To do this inspectors are asked to assess 'the extent to which approaches to financial and resource management help the school to achieve its educational priorities' (Ofsted 2005: 20). This is further amplified to 'the extent to which the school's spending decisions relate to priorities for improvements and benefits for pupils' (2005: 21).

The DEA study of English secondary schools' efficiency was extended by means of a qualitative study into the main features of school leadership and management of a group of peer schools identified as the most efficient for the combination of resources used (Dadd 2006). This showed that efficient schools are distinguished by the overall quality of their leadership and not by the quality of their more narrowly defined financial management. In particular, efficient schools made extensive use of performance data to monitor both student and teacher performance and took action to improve any inadequacies. The schools also had well-worked-out development plans and placed particular emphasis on recruiting high-quality staff. However, apart from a high level of investment in ICT, the schools' environments and learning resources were not in any way outstanding. While the financial administration was sound in routine matters, it was not necessarily run by highly qualified staff or particularly sophisticated.

Conclusion

In this chapter we have focused on evaluating the impact of the budgetary process on the school or college as a whole, but we have also seen that these evaluation techniques, especially benchmarking, are usable for all the sub-units within an organisation. We have seen, however, that there are problems in reconciling the quantitative approaches based on outputs and the qualitative assessments used by teachers as they assess the way in which resources have been used to accord with educational objectives. Problems also result from the dynamic nature of school or college life and the requirement for necessary changes during a budgetary period. We also explored some of the more technical approaches used in the assessment of efficiency and effectiveness in the use of resources, usually at institutional, district or national level. The important message is that evaluation is a necessary part of the budget process and should be planned before spending takes place.

If there is a good evaluation culture within a school or college, the staff will be intuitively aware of the effects produced by particular combinations of resources, even though their costing and assessment of benefits may be imprecise and impressionistic. Evaluation is not something to be undertaken only by the senior leadership group, or finance committee of the governors or council members alone – it can be undertaken by staff at all levels involved in budgetary planning. This may stretch from the secretary responsible for office supplies to the heads of large faculties responsible for a sub-budget used for teaching and ancillary staff, materials of instruction, textbooks and equipment. All staff are part of the whole and all are involved in interpreting the school's vision into programmes of activity that offer alternative approaches to possible outputs and outcomes. As such they are trustees of the school or college and all its assets, the topic of the next chapter.

9 Asset management and capital expenditure

In this chapter we will:

- define key terms such as assets, capital expenditure, investment, depreciation;
- explain the main elements of asset management: replacing depreciated assets and investing in new assets;
- explain investment appraisal methods: pay back and discounted cash flow or net present value, and apply it to a worked example;
- consider how different stakeholders can have differing preferences for investment projects;
- briefly consider the more intensive use of school buildings by means of double shifts.

Asset management

Self-management means that responsibility for the right use of assets rests with the school or college. At the outset, two terms need to be defined:

- Asset: this refers to any item or 'stock' of value that lasts for more than a given period of time (in accounting this is usually more than one year). Assets refer to buildings but also include items of equipment as well as books, as these usually last longer than a year.

• Capital expenditure or investment: this refers to the funds spent (or, in economic terminology, the per period flow of expenditure) on acquiring new assets or on major improvements to existing assets, such as buildings.

In this chapter we will investigate how educational leaders cope with capital as opposed to recurrent (sometimes called revenue) funds. We have already looked at the distinction between the two: recurrent funding tends to be granted on an annual basis for the day-to-day provision of teaching; capital funding is made available on a more sporadic basis for the major changes to the physical assets of the school or college.

Administrators in centralised systems and school and college principals in decentralised systems are concerned with procuring capital assets by securing the adequate and appropriate buildings necessary for effective and efficient teaching.

Few schools and colleges have all of the physical assets they need for their work. Most have a strategic plan so that they can secure the necessary facilities as and when resources become available. As you have seen, the management of revenue resources is subject to the internal policies of the school or college. The management of physical assets may take place through partnering the school community with some form of local or national authority, or it may happen entirely outside the school. In these situations the school or college principals may influence policy but do little to secure the funding necessary for change. Where decentralisation is extensive, as in England and Victoria in Australia, the school receives an annual capital allocation and is responsible for allocating these devolved funds for its own capital programmes with varying degrees of external advice or approval.

The distinction between the funding and management of capital and recurrent resources may suggest that where principals are not involved in managing capital programmes, they may not be as effective a steward of capital resources as those who work in more decentralised systems. The reality is very different. There is a public accountability for the stock of capital that is a school or college. It is expected that users will care for the property. Similarly, although major items of equipment may be externally provided, principals should be involved in assessing need and strategic planning for whole-school improvement. Inevitably, therefore, educational leaders need to have an awareness of the concepts underpinning capital asset management.

Despite the definition of assets being confined to anything that lasts longer than a year, there is a tendency in educational organisations to see capital spending as being related to buildings alone. Increasingly assets include items of information and communications technology equipment that are costly and long-lasting.

The primary aim of asset management is to secure the best possible physical conditions for effective teaching and learning. Whatever the context within which a school or college is working, it best suits its purpose by ensuring that assets are well managed. Good stewardship requires that the school or college should maintain and increase the value of the asset stock.

Depreciation

Schools and colleges are dynamic in nature and their requirements change over time. Over time their assets will decline in value through both wear and tear and obsolescence. This process is called depreciation. Future capital requirements depend in part on the rate at which the existing assets depreciate: for example, five years for a computer, 30 years for a building. Maintenance planning is essential to keep asset values at their maximum, but there will come a time when a building or facility needs to be replaced. In order to manage assets well, the responsible authority (a community, local government, central government or agency for centralised school systems) or the school (in decentralised systems) needs to collect data on the changing value of their capital assets over time. Within the private sector, funds for replacing depreciated assets are usually obtained by setting aside a certain amount so that at the end of the depreciation period adequate replacement funding will be available. Hence depreciation is a cost and is included in the total costs that are subtracted from revenues in order to calculate profit.

In the public sector this has not generally been the practice, and depreciation of assets has not been included as a cost. Consequently the costs of using capital tend to be ignored in the public sector and are treated as having zero cost, even though they do have an often large opportunity cost. The absence in the accounts of the cost of using assets encourages assets to be used without consideration of their costs or of the need to replace them. It is usually anticipated that replacement funding will be available from public sources when required in the future. New Zealand is one of the few countries to include the cost of using capital in their public accounts system and to apply it to schools. In 2000–1, the UK Treasury also adopted 'resource accounting' and now includes the depreciation of public assets in the costs of central government departments. However, resource accounting does not apply to schools in the UK and so they continue not to include depreciation as a cost in their accounts. Even if schools and colleges do not formally include depreciation as a cost in their accounts, it is still important to maintain assets through good care and repair to reduce the rate of depreciation, so long as the maintenance costs do not exceed the cost of replacement. It is also necessary to plan for replacement so that when the asset finally wears out or becomes obsolete there is money in the budget to replace it.

Maintaining existing assets

This means that there should be regular inspections of the property, preferably with the help of a buildings expert. This expert should not have a pecuniary interest in a recommendation to undertake a particular maintenance job, for example, by recommending a building company owned by a relative. It is necessary to judge whether the work should be started immediately or left until funds are available. At this point the opportunity costs of the whole programme of building have to be taken into account. Not only is it a matter of deciding whether it would be better to replace a window frame or rewire a classroom, but the implications of not doing something have to be taken into account. The minimal dangers of a student perhaps being electrocuted as a result of not rewiring may be offset against the leaky window that allows rain to spoil the only computer in the school!

Maintaining security

You will recall that audit procedures are established to ensure that the property of a school or college is properly stored, used and disposed of at the appropriate time. With so much public property in the hands of the school it is possible for misuse, misappropriation and fraud to occur. Asset stocks are best maintained by ensuring good records, clear staff responsibility and regular checks to ensure that misuse does not occur. The cost of lockable storage may well be recouped by the additional security it provides for easily portable items of equipment. It is also important for assets to be insured, provided that the cost of the premiums does not exceed the expected value of any losses that might be incurred. In countries with an active insurance market it is advisable to shop around for the best insurance terms.

Disposal of assets

There are times when the school or college will have assets that have reached the end of their life span or are no longer needed for the school because of changes in the curriculum. Decision-making about disposal needs to be undertaken by more than one person so that there can be no accusation of fraudulent activity. Good practice dictates that where disposal of an asset which still has some life is concerned every effort should be made to place it elsewhere in the education system or to secure some financial rewards if it is disposed of commercially.

Replacement of assets

There is always pressure on resources and the need to purchase new developments may inhibit the planned replacement of equipment, routine repair to property or regular grounds maintenance. When these are postponed, the likelihood of increased expenditure in the future has to be offset against postponement at this stage. Asset management is most effective if those items likely to need replacing are charted in an asset management plan. This recognises not only that assets have a limited life span, but also that where technological progress is rapid and affordable, it may be necessary to replace existing items before the end of their original anticipated life span. This has been evident in schools in England where the installation of interactive whiteboards has affected asset management plans, as shown in this extract from a report to governors on the asset management plan of a school for 750 secondary (11–16) pupils in 2003.

Interactive whiteboards

In each of the past three years the school has equipped one room in each of its five faculties with interactive whiteboard (IWB) technology. This requires a data projector, an associated computer and an electronic screen at a total cost to the school of £2,200 per room. During this initial phase teachers have been introduced to the technology and made aware of associated software that can enhance understanding (for example, the geometry drawing package). Teachers who do not have ready access to this technology have now requested that the equipment should be made available in every room. We believe that there are strong reasons for supporting this as a priority item in the plan for the coming two years. Re-equipping 14 rooms will cost £30,800 per year.

Cost 2003–4   £30,800
Cost 2004–5   £30,800

The changed technology will have an impact on the existing plans. We no longer feel that it is necessary to continue the rolling programme of replacing existing worn non-interactive whiteboards that have badly scratched surfaces and we propose that these should all be removed within the coming four years. This will save £2,600 per year.

Recouped 2003–4 £2,600
Recouped 2004–5 £2,600

Subject departments have agreed to fund the costs of the software through individual departmental budgets and asset plans.
Additional funding for IWB sets will require changes to overall purchasing priorities according to the following proposals:

2003–4

- Saving from computer technology replacement budget (because of lower per unit cost) £3,600

- Saving from refurbishment of laboratory areas (because of redecoration included within the installation of interactive whiteboard budget) £5,200

- Grant from parent-teacher association following change in their pattern of priorities £19,400

Overall asset changes

By 2005 there will be an IWB system in every classroom, and traditional whiteboards will have been removed.

Long-term implications

IWB maintenance will be very limited until 2008 and then five of the original units will have to be replaced at a cost of £11,200.

Planning new asset acquisitions

In most schools and colleges there is usually a long list of the new assets that teachers would like to have available if funding allowed. Adequate asset management requires that these items are identified and then incorporated into strategic planning.

The development of asset plans at every level within a school, college or district allows educational resource use to be maximised. In some countries it is left to local communities to react to the demand for improvements in the overall level of provision, or to agencies to anticipate that demand. In others, local authorities plan and implement provision in response to demand. Whatever the means of funding, three criteria are used in analysis of assets:

- Condition: the physical state of premises and equipment to ensure safe and continuous operation within local and national building regulations.

- Sufficiency: assessing whether the quantity of assets is adequate, for example, are there enough classrooms for the anticipated number of students or, on the other hand, is there surplus capacity that should be removed?

- Suitability: are the buildings and equipment suitable for students' learning needs given the requirements of the provision curriculum, for example, science accommodation, ICT facilities?

A local education authority or district asset management plan is likely to concentrate on the provision of educational places, although there will also be a capital maintenance plan for those elements of building care that are not delegated to individual schools or colleges. In order to compile the plan, it will need to collect the details of every building for which it is responsible and aggregate these plans to assess and evaluate capital maintenance costs in the area concerned. The devolution of funds to schools in some countries now includes some element of capital funding and so asset management planning at school level has become more common.

At district level, asset management planning may set a framework within which school facilities will be developed. The DfES in England set these aims to:

- raise standards of educational achievement;

- provide sustainable and energy-efficient buildings;

- provide innovative design solutions which reflect the needs of ICT-based education;

- increase community use of school facilities;

- maximise value for money;

- ensure efficient and effective management of new and existing capital assets.

Schools and colleges exist within this framework and have to make their own plans to accord with these agreed aims. The process for the development of a school asset management plan includes:

- audit – assisted by buildings, ICT or other specialist advisers to assess resources according to condition, sufficiency and suitability;

- determining priorities – decision-making depends upon local arrangements but should be in accordance with stated educational priorities for the school or college set out in the three-year or other strategic plans;

- feasibility studies – the long-term implications of capital investment are such that full details are required to ensure that the plans are necessary, realistic and properly costed;

- implementation, review and evaluation are necessary to ensure that future asset management plans are based upon an assessment of past practice and provide an opportunity for reviewing the impact of asset planning on educational development.

Costing new student places

The issues looked at above can be made more concrete by considering the example of costing the provision of new student places, which requires a range of additional resources. Beynon (1997) argues that in balancing cost and potential benefit, administrators have to take account of the costs of site purchase, site development and building construction. They then have to add costs for furniture (5–10 per cent of building cost), equipment and electronic infrastructure (now up to 30 per cent of building cost), design fees (up to 6 per cent in a highly competitive market), contingencies (usually 5 per cent of building cost) and an element for inflation between planning and completion stages. He further contends that benchmarking for progress of a scheme against similar schemes requires computing:

- area per place – total building area/total number of pupils;
- cost per area – total cost/total area;
- cost per place – cost per area/area per place.

The major advantage of this approach is that it 'encompasses educational quality considerations as expressed through area per pupil, and construction quality considerations as expressed through cost per unit area' (Beynon 1997: 45). If area per place is reduced, the potential for reduced educational provision is obvious; if cost per unit area is reduced, then the long-term predictions of maintenance need become greater.

Investment appraisal

Investment appraisal is a formal procedure for determining whether a proposed investment in new capital assets is worthwhile. Investing funds in one project means that they are not available for another project. Whether an investment is worth undertaking or not depends on:

- the cost of borrowing the funds needed for the work – the rate of interest;

- the length of time for which the funds are required;

- the potential value of the asset at the end of the investment period – it may have been totally 'consumed' or it may have residual value;

- the anticipated benefits that are obtained from using the asset over its lifetime;

- the risk associated with the costs and benefits (that is, the probability that the costs will be higher than expected and the benefits lower).

A funding authority has several techniques of appraisal available to it. However, in the world of education, public authorities generally receive no monetary income from their investment. They can estimate the costs of undertaking a project against the potentially higher costs of not undertaking the work, for example, overcrowding in the remaining schools, poorer results and poorer educational experience. For them calculations are made on the basis of notional alternative costs.

Public–private partnership schools operate in a system where calculations can be made on anticipated profit. The investors are commercial groups who have been contracted to make educational provision as part of a public–private partnership (PPP). The basic principle for such partnerships, sometimes called private finance initiatives (PFI), is that the company designs, builds and maintains the buildings and leases them back either to the school or the local authority for a specified number of years. In this way the funding authority spreads the capital costs and the rental income offers financial motivation to the providing group.

There are two main methods of investment appraisal: payback and discounted cash flow. Payback is the simpler method. This estimates how many years it would take for the income from a project to cover the cost of the investment (the initial cost plus interest), and investors make a decision on that basis. The shorter the payback period, the more attractive the investment. However, the payback method is crude and does not take into account the fact that a given amount of money today is worth more than the same amount in one or several years' time.

The advantage of the *discounted cash flow* (DCF) method is that it recognises that investment in assets has an opportunity cost. If money is used to purchase a capital asset, it is 'locked up' and cannot be used to purchase a recurrent resource or invested in a bank or national savings, for example, and earn interest. The discounted cash flow method is a way of working out if the return on an investment is expected to be greater or less than the rate of interest that could be earned from a financial asset. This is done by comparing the expected present value of the returns from the investment with the amount of money that has to be invested in the present in order to buy physical assets.

The simplest approach to the idea of discounting is to consider it as the opposite calculation to the familiar compound interest formula. With compound interest, if you invest £100 at 10 per cent for one year, at the end of year one it will be worth $100(1+0.1) = 100 + 10 = 110$.

If you invest the money for a further year and let the interest accumulate, then after two years you will have $110(1+0.1) = 110 + 11 = 121$.

This is the same as $100(1+0.1)(1+0.1) = 100(1+0.1)2$.

The general expression for the value of £1 after it has been invested for t years at a rate of interest of r is $1(1+r)t$
where:
r = rate of interest expressed as a decimal
t = the number of years of which interest is reinvested.

Present value

If the rate of interest is 10 per cent then there would be no difference between having £100 now and having £110 in one year's time. This is because if the person receives £100 now they can invest it at 10 per cent and get £110 in one year's time. If they need the money now, then they could sell their claim to £110 in one year's time to someone who is happy to wait a year for £110 in return for paying £100 for the claim to £110 in one year's time.

Hence the present value of £110 received in a year's time when the rate of interest is 10 per cent is £100. To calculate the net present value of £110 in one year we then need to do the reverse calculation to compound interest.

We *divide* £110 by (1+0.1), i.e. by 1.1 to get £100.

This is the same as dividing by (1+0.1)t = (1+0.1)1 since t = 1.

To calculate the present value of £121 in two years' time when r = 0.1 we divide by (1+0.1)2 = 1.21. Of course £121/1.21 is £100.

Therefore the general expression for the present value of a sum of money £Ct received in t years' time is:

$$PV = \frac{C_t}{(1 + r)^t}$$

If several amounts of money Ct are received in different years one, two and three up to year t then the present value of this cash flow is:

$$PV = \frac{C_1}{(1 + r)^1} + \frac{C_2}{(1 + r)^2} + \frac{C_3}{(1 + r)^3} + \dots + \frac{C_t}{(1 + r)^t}$$

This is written with a summation sign as:

$$PV = \sum_{t=1}^{t=T} \frac{C_t}{(1 + r)^t}$$

where:

Ct = the cash return from the asset in year t

r = the rate of interest or rate of discount.

The interest rate 'r' when used to calculate the present value of the sum of money due to be received in the future is known as the *rate of discount*. The procedure of calculating the present value of a future sum of money is known as discounting.

The present value of a stream of cash flows anticipated from an investment can be calculated using a present value table. In Table 9.1 we show part of a present value table for 20 years and for interest rates from 1 per cent to 12 per cent. Each row gives the present value of £1 after one, two and up to 20 years and each column gives the present value of £1 for a specified discount rate.

When using the discounted cash flow method to appraise an investment proposal, the rule is that a 'positive net present value' indicates that the value of the net cash flows from the investment is greater than the value of the alternative investment that yields the discount rate (i.e. the rate of interest on alternative investments in the capital market).

A public sector version of discounted flow investment appraisal, when the returns are not in the form of cash revenues, is cost-benefit analysis – where methods for valuing benefits that do not have market prices are used.

Table 9.1 Present value of £100 in year t at interest rate r

Discount rate (r) %	1%	2%	3%	4%	5%	6%	7%	8%	9%	10%
Present value of £1 in 1 year's time is 1/(1+r)	0.99	0.98	0.97	0.96	0.95	0.94	0.93	0.93	0.92	0.91
Year = t	All these cells are 100* (1 / (1 + r)t)									
1	99.01	98.04	97.09	96.15	95.24	94.34	93.46	92.59	91.74	90.91
2	98.03	96.12	94.26	92.46	90.70	89.00	87.34	85.73	84.17	82.64
3	97.06	94.23	91.51	88.90	86.38	83.96	81.63	79.38	77.22	75.13
4	96.10	92.38	88.85	85.48	82.27	79.21	76.29	73.50	70.84	68.30
5	95.15	90.57	86.26	82.19	78.35	74.73	71.30	68.06	64.99	62.09
6	94.20	88.80	83.75	79.03	74.62	70.50	66.63	63.02	59.63	56.45
7	93.27	87.06	81.31	75.99	71.07	66.51	62.27	58.35	54.70	51.32
8	92.35	85.35	78.94	73.07	67.68	62.74	58.20	54.03	50.19	46.65
9	91.43	83.68	76.64	70.26	64.46	59.19	54.39	50.02	46.04	42.41
10	90.53	82.03	74.41	67.56	61.39	55.84	50.83	46.32	42.24	38.55
11	89.63	80.43	72.24	64.96	58.47	52.68	47.51	42.89	38.75	35.05
12	88.74	78.85	70.14	62.46	55.68	49.70	44.40	39.71	35.55	31.86
13	87.87	77.30	68.10	60.06	53.03	46.88	41.50	36.77	32.62	28.97
14	87.00	75.79	66.11	57.75	50.51	44.23	38.78	34.05	29.92	26.33

Table 9.1 Present value of £100 in year t at interest rate r (cont'd)

Discount rate (r) %	1%	2%	3%	4%	5%	6%	7%	8%	9%	10%
Present value of £1 in 1 year's time is 1/(1+r)	0.99	0.98	0.97	0.96	0.95	0.94	0.93	0.93	0.92	0.91
Year = t	All these cells are $100*(1/(1+r)^t)$									
15	86.13	74.30	64.19	55.53	48.10	41.73	36.24	31.52	27.45	23.94
16	85.28	72.84	62.32	53.39	45.81	39.36	33.87	29.19	25.19	21.76
17	84.44	71.42	60.50	51.34	43.63	37.14	31.66	27.03	23.11	19.78
18	83.60	70.02	58.74	49.36	41.55	35.03	29.59	25.02	21.20	17.99
19	82.77	68.64	57.03	47.46	39.57	33.05	27.65	23.17	19.45	16.35
20	81.95	67.30	55.37	45.64	37.69	31.18	25.84	21.45	17.84	14.86

The application of investment appraisal systems

Investment appraisal has been used as a vital tool in the decision-making armoury of public services for at least 30 years as a means of assessing the effects of expenditure. Analysis is structured to consider the costs in necessary capital, other resources and labour inputs and relate these to intended outcomes, be they measurable, such as examination results, or non-measurable, such as improved ethos.

In Chapter 8 we introduced two evaluation methods for investment used in the public sector: cost-benefit analysis (CBA) and cost-effectiveness analysis (CEA). We did not mention that both involve calculating the present value of costs and benefits, although CEA is used when a monetary value cannot be attached to the benefits but only to the costs. With CEA it is only possible to compare investments that produce outputs that can be measured in the same units, for example, gains in a reading test. If the benefits can be valued in money terms then different investment possibilities can be assessed using CBA. For example, the purchase of a multi-function photocopier might save the reprographics assistant's time and so the benefit can be valued in money terms. Nicol and Coen (2003) offer a model for ascertaining cost-benefit and cost-effectiveness at institutional level for all information and communications technology within higher education contexts. They point to issues of availability, full-time use and access for both students and teachers in a more effective way than through conventional book-based knowledge management systems. This is still subjective in part but attempts to enhance cost-benefit understanding through attaching values to cost-effectiveness data.

However, it is also essential to recognise that the 'costs' might include some non-quantifiable elements such as:

- an increase in materials used as staff become aware of the system;

- stress on the part of the assistant working under greater pressure;

- the costs of monitoring use so that there can be a re-charge to departments.

In assessing benefit it is not always possible to put a money value on a project and so do a CBA, but it is possible to assess what kinds of benefits are likely and how important they are, and in this way to do a systematic appraisal.

Case study 3: Costing the use of capital equipment: the cost of an ICT lesson

Knowing how to discount to obtain net present values is a useful technique for managers who are costing investments in schools and colleges. It also enables them to calculate how to include depreciation costs into the total costs of a project. The following illustration shows this at work.

Greenside School is considering investing in a new computer suite (a dedicated classroom with 30 work stations). Evaluation involves costing a one-hour lesson. This will assist policy decisions in three ways by:

- comparing ICT lesson costs with other subjects in order to decide which should receive priority in expenditure planning;

- deciding what is a reasonable charge for external users of the computer suite;

- comparing the costs of purchasing and renting equipment. Calculations are made in two steps:

Step 1: identifying all the relevant cost ingredients;

Step 2: having identified the cost ingredients, work out the cost per lesson hour of each ingredient. This enables the cost of an hour of computer use to be calculated, which is the main focus of the exercise. In Table 9.2 the question mark in the bottom right-hand cell indicates that this cost is what we want to work out.

Overall assumptions for costing:

- School timetable: 25 one-hour periods a week

- School open: 39 weeks a year

- Computer suite used: 38 weeks a year

Assumptions about computer costs

There are two opportunity costs associated with using the computers over five years:

- £18,000 is forgone in depreciation of the equipment over five years;

- the opportunity cost of the interest rate that could have been earned on £18,000 if it had not been spent on computers but invested. This is assumed to be 5 per cent per annum.

Costing method 1: Entering depreciation and interest costs in the year they occur

Assumption: the computers depreciate at 50 per cent per annum over five years. In the fifth year, the value falls by slightly more, so that the resale value of the computers will be zero.

Table 9.2   Calculating the cost per lesson hour in a new computer suite

Ingredient	Unit cost	Assumptions	Cost per lesson hour
Teacher time	£29,812 per year (including National Insurance and pension contributions)	Assume cost 25 hours per week for 40 weeks	£30
Technician time	£13,650 a year or £10 an hour	Works 35 hours per week for 39 weeks: 10 hours a week on new computer suite.	£5
Professional development for staff	£360 per staff member per year	3 teachers and 1 technician included (total staffing for the week)	£0.50
Telephone costs	Zero	Lump sum fee already paid for unlimited access	£0
Stationery, etc.	£760 per computer room		£1.00
Room occupancy	Occupation and admin costs for school = £360,000 p.a.	Occupancy rate of room per week is 80%. Room takes up 1/60 of total area of school buildings	£15.00
Software licences	£760 a year for 30 extra computers	Paid annually	£1.00
Insurance, maintenance	£1,500 pa		£2.00
30 PCs and laser printer	£18,000 (purchased)	Will last for 5 years, at end of which no resale value	?

Table 9.3   Costing the use of computers to include the cost of depreciation in the year it occurs

	Year 1	Year 2	Year 3	Year 4	Year 5	Total over 5 years
Annual depreciation @ 0.5	9,000 (18,000*0.5)	4,500 (9,000*0.5)	2,250 (4,500*.5)	1,125 (2,250*0.5)	1,125 (1,125*1)	18,000
End-of year-resale value of computers (value at beginning of year minus depreciation)	9,000 (18,000 –9,000)	4,500 (9,000 –4,500)	2,250 (4,500 –2,250)	1,125 (2,250 –1,125)	0 (1,125 –1,125)	
Resource use cost per annum (value at beginning of year minus at end of year)	9,000	4,500	2,250	1,125	1,125	18,000
Annual interest payments forgone (Value of money invested in computers x rate of interest)	900 (18,000* 0.05)	450 (9,000* 0.05)	225 (4,500* 0.05)	112.5 (2,250* 0.05)	56.25 (1,125* 0.05)	1,744
Total opportunity cost of computer use	9,900	4,950	2,475	1,238	1,181	19,744

The first row in Table 9.3 shows the annual depreciation of the computers given that they depreciate at an annual rate of 50 per cent of their value at the beginning of the year. The second row gives the value of the computers at the end of the year – depreciation has been subtracted. The third row is the resource use cost of the computers. This is the same as their depreciation – the amount of value used up in the course of the year. The fourth row is the interest earnings forgone by the school because they invested £18,000 in computers and not in a financial asset. The total opportunity cost of using the computers is the amounts in rows 4 and 5 (resource use cost plus forgone interest).

Costing method 2: Equivalent annuity – spreading the cost of computer usage over five years

Step 1: Work out opportunity cost of investing £18,000 in a computer suite for five years: this is the compound interest earned on £18,000 invested at 5 per cent for five years with £18,000 returned at the end of the fifth year.

Interest receipts in year 1 = 18,000*0.05 = 900
Interest receipts t in year 2 = (1,800 + 900)*0.05 = 945
Interest receipts in year 3 = (1,800 + 945)*0.05 = 992
Interest receipts in year 4 = (1,800 + 992)*0.05 = 1,042
Interest receipts in year 5 = (1,800 + 1,042) = 1,094 plus £18,000 returned.

The cash flow is therefore zero money for years one to four, and then all the interest payments that were reinvested, which add up to £4,973 plus £18,000 principal. The total is £22,973.

Step 2: Work out the annuity. An annuity is a financial asset that pays a constant annual income for a given number of years. For the computer problem it is necessary to calculate what constant sum of money received every year for five years and reinvested at 5 per cent per annum would be worth the same to the school as £18,000 invested at the beginning of year one at 5 per cent for five years.

If the interest rate were 5 per cent, you would be indifferent between:

- having £18,000 now which you invest at 5 per cent compound interest for five years which gives you £22,973 at the end of year five, and

- receiving an annuity of £x per year for four years, reinvesting it at compound interest of 5 per cent per annum so as to obtain £22,973 in five years' time.

To calculate the equivalent annuity we need to work out what constant sum of money, £x, received in each year for five years and invested at 5 per cent compound interest would accumulate to $22,973 after five years. This can be found out using an annuity table. This annuity is £4,158 per annum. The equivalence between (A) and (B) is shown in Table 9.4.

Hence, the *annualised opportunity cost of spending £18,000* on computers with zero value after five years is £4,158. This is because an annual income of £4,158 per annum over five years would give the school the same amount of money in the bank after five years as starting in the first year with £18,000 and investing at compound interest of 5 per cent for five years.

Hence the cost of using the computers is £4,158 a year if you use a constant per annum cost.

Table 9.4 Comparing investing £18,000 for five years with an annuity giving £4,158 per annum for five years

	Year 1	Year 2	Year 3	Year 4	Year 5	Total over 5 years
Interest payments on £18,000 invested for 5 years @ 5% compound interest	900	945	992	1,042	1,094	4,973
Total sum received for investing £18,000 for 5 years at 5% compound interest	0	0	0	0	0	4,973 + 18,000 = 22,973
Annuity						
Interest income from having an annual income of £4,158 reinvested for 5 years @ 5%		208	426	655	896	2,186
Total sum received at end of 5 years with reinvested interest income on an annuity of £4,158 p.a.						= 5*4,158 + 2,186 = 20,790 + 2,186 = 22,976

(Note: rounding errors account for the £3 difference in the two sums.)

Annualised cost of computer usage per hour

If we take the annual cost of the computers as £4,158, then the cost of usage for computers for an hour is (4,158/(20 x 38)) = £5.50.

Look back to Table 9.2 and enter £5.50 in the bottom right-hand cell. Totalling up all the cost ingredients, we arrive at £60 as the cost per lesson hour. For hiring out the computer suite, the school should charge at least £27.50 to cover room provision, computer depreciation, technician, insurance and maintenance.

While complex, and possibly daunting, this lengthy calculation offers a way forward for those schools now managing their own capital resources and needing to know how they can best meet the costs of the effective support of new technology as a recurrent cost factor.

Stewardship of assets – whose school is it anyway?

If decisions for or against investment are to be made without unfair pressure from each of the stakeholder groups, rationality is required for the use of capital as well as for recurrent expenditure. This is achieved through project appraisal. Alternative plans that include full identification of costs and benefits can be evaluated against the aims and objectives of the school or college. However, decisions are subject to a number of pressures and rationality may be compromised.

We have already indicated the importance of liaison with school or college stakeholders. These include all those who have an interest in a school or college because they pay taxes or local taxes for education, those who attend the school and their parents, the community who might use facilities and the employers who will use students, and so on. The political and lobbying power of stakeholders may well affect decision-making. The community responsible for Ubuntu School in a developing area of southern Africa was faced with securing capital for asset improvement – but there were a number of influences at work.

The school is a large primary school with 420 pupils on roll serving a suburban area with good community support. It has eight classrooms, but since 2000 it has been under pressure to expand and has asked its district for more financial help. While there is willingness to consider the provision of an additional room, there is also some local feeling that the school is not living up to its title (which means 'our shared humanity') and aim of openness. Parents have offered to help in maintaining the existing rooms that clearly show wear-and-tear, but the headteacher has turned this down, fearing that the district will then expect the parents to build the additional room. The community health group would like to make more use of the facilities, but the headteacher has declined to help because providing for other groups would indicate that there was surplus space in the building for some of the time. The teachers have argued that they need some sort of secure base for holding the scarce scientific and computer resources and feel that, following a recent spate of local thefts, this is of higher priority than an additional room, but the headteacher has responded by suggesting that one more teaching room would reduce the pressure on existing facilities and could allow for a secure storage facility in every room.

Making more efficient use of buildings when space is limited

This ownership by stakeholders is more marked in countries where the community finances the school and actually helps to build and maintain it. The community has a very real interest as stakeholders and accordingly exerts an influence on policy. Often their greatest problem is one of pressure on accommodation.

Where this occurs and the cost of a new building is prohibitive, two courses of action are available:

- The use of double or even treble shifts so that school buildings are used for much more than the traditional five hours per day. This has advantages in that the capital is intensively used and revenue is increased where fee income (however small) is required, but there are disadvantages in different groups of staff using the premises and increased pressure on the infrastructure and equipment.

- The arrangement of the school year so that the buildings are used throughout the year with minimal closure. This has advantages where the basic work of the school continues in normal term time and support or community teaching takes place in traditional holiday periods – the two groups coexist. There are disadvantages where students have a long break between periods of attendance. Also, where the system is used, there is a tendency to go for two parallel groups of students attending for three days each week. Again pressures on accommodation, infrastructure and teaching equipment are considerable, but it is argued that the 'part-time' nature of schooling still allows for traditional youth employment in agriculture.

Linden (2001) puts double shift work into perspective by showing that it is not simply a matter of more intensive use of capital assets but that the quality of educational experience has to be taken into account. He is careful to distinguish the reasoning behind multiple use of premises: is it to optimise capital use, maximise student throughput, or to maximise fee or grant per student income? He suggests that common motivation for double shift organisation may vary as follows:

- increased efficiency of use of human and capital resources (i.e. teachers can teach more pupils and there is a reduced need to build more schools);

- increased access through increased number of school places;

- increased teacher salaries without increasing unit costs, if salaries are low and teachers are paid only a little more per shift for teaching two shifts;

- pupils can perform productive work during the day (because they attend school only in the morning, afternoon or night), thus reducing the opportunity costs of attending schooling;

- where enrolment rates are high, overcrowding is reduced.

However, there are costs as detailed below.

> One of the principal reasons for moving to a double-shift arrangement is the potential savings from not having to build more schools to accommodate increased numbers of pupils. There are, in fact, very few studies able or that even attempt to substantiate this claim. A study in Malaysia did calculate *capital* savings of 25% for secondary schools. One might hypothesise that savings at the secondary level are especially important (and desirable) to achieve because of the high cost of science, computers, and other specialist equipment.
>
> (Linden 2001: 3)

Savings on *recurrent* budget costs depend on the specific organisation of schools. For example, no recurrent expenditure savings will accrue if two sets of teachers are used (as happened in Zimbabwe) or if teachers are paid twice as much for teaching a second shift. However, in Senegal those working a second shift are only paid an extra 25 per cent. Similarly, a single headteacher for both 'schools' would save money if they are not paid twice as much. Hypothetically, more effective use of administrative staff, such as guards and messengers, can also be made, although there appear to be no studies attempting to demonstrate or quantify this.

It should be noted, however, that

> 'double-shifting' is likely to place increased burdens on school facilities, which is likely to lead to higher *maintenance* costs and reduced life span. This is especially pertinent in poor countries where the facilities may be in poor condition to begin with. Again, though, there is no documentation of the magnitude of these changes or the extent to which they outweigh potential savings.
>
> (Linden 2001: 5)

Above all, Linden points to the fact that unless there are capacity reasons for undertaking double shifts, there is no evidence of cognitive or other outcome advantages.

Conclusion

This chapter has introduced several aspects of managing assets within schools and colleges. Some sections may have been difficult for readers who lack mathematical understanding, but we included them because they can be useful to those who wish to do more realistic costings that take account of capital costs. The costing exercises reveal the complexity of financial and resource management. It is not simply a matter of securing resources for here and now, but rather of recognising that some resources last a long time and can be made to last longer with appropriate management. Resources are an essential part of the educational process and they must be used with care, programmed into the budget and management plans for the school, and evaluated for their part in helping the organisation achieve its stated aims and objectives.

There is an interesting debate concerning the place of new technologies in the educational process and this could be shifting some of the traditional balances in education funding away from human capital in staffing to investment in physical capital in equipment.

Dadd (2006) found that one feature of efficient English secondary schools was that they invested heavily in ICT for learning purposes. Another example is schools in Mexico that are being equipped with new technology so that the curriculum content, delivery and assessment for secondary schools can be nationally organised in the context of attempts to devolve management to the school level. In our final chapter we explore some of these growing tensions a little further.

10 Conclusions

This is a brief, but important chapter that brings together the main threads of our argument that educational resource management requires an understanding of the open systems environment, strategic and budgetary planning, and evaluation of processes, outputs and outcomes. This will, we argue, help to ensure that financial resources are used effectively, efficiently and in a way that is both equitable and provides value for money.

Managing finances and resources for educational organisations is a challenging task. The outputs and outcomes of educational organisations are multiple and have both private and public benefits. There are many different stakeholders with different interests in how resources are used. Ambiguities in relating inputs to consequent educational outputs and outcomes make it difficult to measure efficiency in education. Equity and efficiency, though difficult to make operational, are used as the main criteria for assessing how education is funded and how its provision is divided between public and private sector organisations.

In most environments educational practice is lacking in some ways, for example, through incomplete planning, pragmatic rather than planned resource use, casual control systems and a failure to listen to the voice of stakeholders. Because of criticism of public sector inefficiency, government policy in many countries has been increasingly concerned not just with how much is spent on education but on establishing funding systems that promote equity and that contain appropriate incentives for educational organisations to manage their resources efficiently. A marked trend has been towards formula funding based, in large part, on student numbers so that funding is demand led and gives incentives to providers to perform well. Decentralised budgeting has also been encouraged on the principle that local managers are better informed about local needs and costs than those at the centre. In both developing – and even developed – countries mixed public and private funding has become more prevalent as educational institutions are encouraged to raise some of their own resources both to ease the tax collection burden on the state and to ensure that students and parents have incentives to demand good-quality education from providers.

However, a number of potential tensions remain and affect the way in which policy makers and those putting policy into effect perceive their task.

Efficiency incentives may harm equity. For example, they give schools and colleges an incentive to recruit students who are less costly to educate, and private sources of funding inevitably lead to differential quality linked to income. This may affect the opportunities of those with special learning needs or those with disabilities of some sort.

Because of the increasing political importance of education, governments still wish to intervene to achieve specific policy outcomes, despite promoting decentralised budget management as a means to enhanced efficiency. As a result, schools and colleges lack the freedom to work creatively to establish their vision because of national requirements in curriculum planning or examination structures.

There are tensions between the desire for national cohesion via uniform public education and private demands for differentiated education.

In a world where public sector educational organisations are experiencing greater degrees of financial autonomy, with its increased uncertainties and opportunities, educational managers need to cope both strategically with the impact of these policy tensions on their organisation as well as attend to the careful details of day-to-day budget management. To some extent a 'law of unintended consequences' (Liefner 2003: 470) operates, such as where breadth of education is sacrificed so that measurable outcomes, for example, examination results, can secure recruitment for schools or courses. Liefner (2003) considered these consequences within higher education and noted that the behaviour of academics and managers has changed to the point where they are less ready to undertake risk activity in developing their departments and, as a result, research objectives are tied more closely to national policy requirements and teaching accords with course completion criteria. His argument is that educational creativity may be stifled for fear of lack of resource allocation, either from student fees or from bid income.

Going further

There has been considerable research in recent years into many aspects of effectiveness, efficiency, equity and value for money in resource management on a local or national scale. This is recorded in the contents pages of the following journals:

Economics of Education Review
Journal of Educational Administration
Education Economics

There is also considerable material to be found in the discussion papers from the University of York, UK.

A wealth of material from the USA is available either from the ERIC Clearing House on the internet, or from the Department of Educational Statistics in Washington. A major centre for the study of school finance is the Consortium for Policy Research in Education at the University of Wisconsin-Madison (http://www.wcer.wise.edu/cpre).

Regional materials based on research are also available from the World Bank, UNESCO, the European Commission, and Organisation for Economic and Cultural Development – the publication lists for all of these can be found on the internet . Your own national educational departments and statistical bureaus may well make their research materials available on the internet.

However, so much of this work is concerned with the macro-economics – the big picture – which tells us a great deal about the relationship between national and district systems and educational outcomes. As workers in the research field, we have had to dig long and deep to find examples of the micro-economics of education – the way things work at the local school or college level. Management and leadership issues are considered in the following international journals – they do not always reveal the detail of policy implication, but outline the main issues surrounding resources:

School Leadership and Management
Educational Management and Administration
International Journal of Educational Management

as well as local educational journals.

If you recognise that no system is perfect, no two contexts and no two sets of pressures are the same, there will be widespread differences in practice. For us, the important issue is that of awareness so that leaders and managers within schools, colleges and university departments can speak with understanding about educational resource issues.

References

Ansoff, L. (1987) *Corporate Strategy*. Harmondsworth: Penguin Books.

Anderson, L. (2000) 'The move towards entrepreneurialism'. In M. Colman and L. Anderson (eds) *Managing Finance and Resources in Education*. London: Paul Chapman Press.

Anthony, A.E. and Herzlinger, R.E. (1989) 'Management control in non-profit organisations'. In R. Levačić (ed.) *Financial Management in Education*. Buckingham: Open University Press.

Audit Commission (1984) *Code of Local Government Audit Practice for England and Wales*. London: HMSO.

Audit Commission (1993, revised 2000) *Keeping your Balance*. London: HMSO.

Audit Commission/DfES (2000, revised 2005) *Getting the Best From Your Budget: A Guide to Effective Management of School Resources*. London: The Stationery Office.

Bailey, A. and Johnson, G. (1997) 'How strategies develop in organisations'. In M. Preedy, R. Glatter and R. Levačić (eds) *Educational Management: Strategy, Quality and Resources*. Buckingham: Open University Press.

Baines, E. (2000) 'Managing information as a resource'. In M. Coleman and L. Anderson (eds) *Managing Finance and Resources in Education*. London: Paul Chapman Press.

Barr, N. and Crawford, I. (2005) *Financing Higher Education: Answers from the UK*. London: Routledge.

Bedi, S. and Edwards, J.H. (2002) 'The impact of school quality on earnings and educational returns – evidence from a low income country'. *Journal of Development Economics* 68, 157–61 and 182–3.

Benson, E.D. and Marks, B.R. (2005) ' "Robin Hood" and Texas School District borrowing costs'. *Public Budgeting and Finance* 25 (2), 84.

Berne, R. and Stiefel, L. (1995) *Student Level Resource Measures: Selected Papers in School Finance.* Washington, DC: National Center for Educational Statistics.

Beynon, J. (1997) *Physical Facilities for Education: What Planners Need to Know.* Paris: Unesco International Institute for Educational Planning.

Bush, T. (2003) 'Change management styles: impact on finance and resources'. In M. Coleman and L. Anderson (eds) *Managing Finance in Education.* London: Paul Chapman Press.

Bush, T., Coleman, M. and Glover, D. (1993) *Managing Autonomous Schools.* London: Paul Chapman Press.

Butler, J. (1991) 'Toward understanding and measuring conditions of trust: evolution of a conditions of trust inventory'. *Journal of Management* 17 (3), 643–63.

Caldwell, B. (2002) 'Autonomy and self-management: concepts and evidence'. In T. Bush and L. Bell *The Principles and Practices of Educational Management.* London: Paul Chapman Press.

Caldwell, B.J. and Spinks, J.M. (1988) *The Self-managing School.* Lewes: Falmer Press.

Caldwell, B.J. and Spinks, J.M. (1992) *Leading the Self-managing School.* Lewes: Falmer Press.

Chiba, A. (2000) *Public Private Partnership in the Social Sector.* Tokyo: Asian Development Bank.

Coleman, M. and Anderson, L. (2000) *Managing Finance and Resources in Education.* London: Paul Chapman Press.

Dadd, A. (2006) *Investigating the Effective Use of Resources in Secondary Schools: Research Report RR799.* London: DfES.

Daun, H. (2004) 'Privatisation, decentralization and governance in education in the Czech Republic, England, France, Germany and Sweden'. *International Review of Education* 50, 325–46.

DfES (2005) *Financial Standards: Introduction to the DfES Financial Management Standards in Schools.* London, DfES.

Edwards, P., Ezzamel, M. and Robson, K. (1999) 'Connecting accounting and education in the UK: discourses and accountability of education reform'. *Critical Perspectives on Accounting* 10, 469–500.

Eurydice (2004) *Diagrams Showing Financial Flows in Compulsory Education in Europe 2001*. Paris: Eurydice.

Glover, D. and Law, S. (2002) 'Graduateness and employability: student perceptions of the personal outcomes of university education'. *Research in Post-compulsory Education* 7 (3), 293–306.

Glover, D., Gleeson, D., Gough, G. and Johnson, M. (1998) 'The meaning of management: the development needs of middle managers in secondary schools'. *Educational Management and Administration* 26 (3), 279–92.

Glover, D., Levačić, R., Bennett, N. and Earley, P. (1996) 'Leadership: planning and resource management in very effective schools'. *School Organisation* 16 (2), 135–48, and 16 (3).

Glyn, J. (1987) *Public Sector Financial Control and Accounting*. Oxford: Blackwell.

Handy, C. (1993) *Understanding Organisations*. Harmondsworth: Penguin Books.

Hanson, E.M. (1998) 'Strategies of educational decentralisation: key questions and core issues'. *Journal of Educational Administration* 36 (2): 111–28.

Hanushek, E. (2006) 'Alternative school policies and the benefits of general cognitive skills'. *Economics of Education Review* 25, 447–62.

Harber, C. and Davies, L. (1998) *School Management and Effectiveness in Developing Countries*. London: Continuum.

HM Treasury (2002) *Managing Resources: Implementing Resource Based Financial Management*. London: HM Treasury (www.hmt.gov.uk).

Jenkins, A., Levačić, R. and Vignoles, A. (2006) *Estimating the Relationship Between School Resources and Pupil Attainment at GSCE*. Nottingham: DfES.

Jones, D. (1987) 'A practical unit cost approach to budgeting and accountability in colleges'. In R. Levačić (ed.) *Financial Management in Education*. Buckingham: Open University Press.

Knight, B. (1993) 'Budgetary control, evaluation and equity'. In *Financial Management for Schools: The Thinking Managers Guide*. Oxford: Heinemann.

Knight, B. (1997) 'Budget analysis and construction'. In M. Preedy, R. Glatter and R. Levačić (eds) *Educational Management: Strategy, Quality and Resources*. Buckingham: Open University Press.

Kremer, M., Moulin, S., Myatt, D. and Namunyu, R. (1997) *The Quality–Quantity Trade Off in Education: Evidence from a Prospective Evaluation in Kenya*. Washington, DC: World Bank and Harvard University.

Levačić, R. (1997) 'Financial and resource management'. In M. Preedy and R. Glatter *Educational Management, Strategy, Quality and Resources*. Buckingham: Open University Press.

Levačić, R. (1999) 'Modern headship for the rationally managed school'. In T. Bush, L. Bell, R. Bolam, R. Glatter and P. Ribbins (eds) *Educational Management: Redefining Theory, Policy and Practice*. London: Paul Chapman Press.

Levačić , R. (2000) 'Linking resources to learning outcomes'. In M. Coleman and L. Anderson (eds) *Managing Finance in Education*. London: Paul Chapman Press.

Levačić, R. (2003) *Financing schools to achieve efficiency and equity: a review of practices and their application to Bosnia and Herzegovina*. Ministry of Education and Culture (Republika Srpska) and Ministry of Education and Science of Federation of Bosnia and Herzegovina.

Levačić, R. and Vignoles, A. (2002) 'Researching the links between school resources and student outcomes in the UK: a review of issues and evidence'. *Education Economics* 10 (3), 312–31.

Levin, H.M. (1987) 'Privatization: theory and practice'. *Journal of Policy Analysis and Management* 6 (4), 628–41.

Levin, H. and McEwan, P. (2001) *Cost Effectiveness Analysis: Methods and Applications*. Thousand Oaks, CA: Sage.

Liefner, I. (2003) 'Funding, resource allocation and performance in higher education systems'. *Higher Education* 46 (4), 469–89.

Linden, T. (2001) *Double Shift Secondary Schools*. Washington, DC: World Bank.

Little, A.W. (2004) *Access and Achievement in Commonwealth Countries: Support for Learning and Teaching in Multigrade Classrooms*. Commonwealth Education Partnerships.

López, M.J.G. (2006) 'Towards decentralized and goal-oriented models of Institutional resource allocation: the Spanish case'. *Higher Education* 51 (4), 589.

McAleese, K. (2000) 'Budgeting in schools'. In M. Coleman and L. Anderson (eds) *Managing Finance and Resources in Education.* London: Paul Chapman Press.

Miller, D.J. and Glover, D. (2006) 'Interactive whiteboard evaluation for the secondary national strategy: developing the use of interactive whiteboards in mathematics'. In *Final Report for the Secondary National Strategy.* London: DfES. Available http://www.standards.dfes.gov.uk/keystage3/ downloads/ma_iaw_eval_rpt.pdf.

Mintzberg, H. (1994) *The Rise and Fall of Strategic Planning.* London: Prentice Hall.

Mintzberg, H. and Quinn, J.B. (1996) *The Strategy Process: Concepts, Contexts, Cases.* London: Prentice Hall.

Muta, H. (2000) 'Deregulation and decentralisation of education in Japan'. *Journal of Educational Administration* 38 (5), 455–67.

Nicol, D. and Coen, M. (2003) 'A model for evaluating the institutional costs and benefits of ICT initiatives in teaching and learning in higher education'. *Association for Learning Technology Journal* 11 (2), 46–60.

Ntshoe, I.M. (2003) 'The political economy of access and equitable allocation of resources to higher education'. *International Journal of Educational Development* 23 (4), 381–98.

Odden, A. and Picus, L. (1992) *School Finance: A Policy Perspective.* New York: McGraw-Hill.

Ofsted (1995) *Handbook of Guidance for Inspection of Secondary Schools.* London: HMSO.

Ofsted (2005) *Every Child Matters: Framework for Inspecting Schools in England.* London: Ofsted.

OECD (2006) *Education at a Glance.* Paris: Unesco.

Penton Media (2007) 'Financial mismanagement'. Dallas, Texas.

Rosenbaum, D. and Lamort, F. (1992) 'Entry barriers, exit and sunk costs: an analysis'. *Applied Economics* 24 (3), 297–304.

Ross, K.N. and Levačić, R. (eds) (1999) *Needs-based Resource Allocation in Education.* Paris: Unesco.

Salerno, C. (2006) 'Using data envelopment analysis to improve estimates of higher education institution's per student education costs'. *Education Economics* 14 (3), 281–95.

Sav, G.T. (2004) 'Higher education costs and scale and scope economies'. *Applied Economics* 36 (6), 607–14.

Scheerens, J. (1997) 'Conceptual models and theory-embedded principles on effective schooling' *School Effectiveness and School Improvement* 8 (3), 269–310.

Scheerens, J. (1999) 'Concepts and theories of school effectiveness'. In A.J. Visscher *Managing Schools Towards High Performance*. Lisse: Swets & Zeitlinger.

Simkins, T. (2000) 'Cost analysis in education'. In M. Coleman and L. Anderson (eds) *Managing Finance in Education*. London: Paul Chapman Press.

Simon, H.A. (1964) 'On the concept of organizational goal'. *Administrative Science Quarterly* 9 (1), 1–22.

Smith, P. C. and Street, A. (2006) *Analysis of Secondary School Efficiency: Final Report: Research Report RR788*. London: DfES.

Swanson, A.D. and King, R.A. (1991) *School Finance: Its Economics and Politics*. Harlow: Longman.

Tao, H.L. and Yuan, M.C. (2005) 'Optimal scale of a public elementary school with commuting costs? A case study of Taipei county'. *Economics of Education Review* 24 (4), 407.

Tiebout, C. (1956) 'A pure theory of local government expenditure'. *Journal of Political Economy* 64, 416–24.

Tooley, J. and Dixon, P. (2005) 'An inspector calls: the regulation of "budget" private schools in Hyderabad, Andhra Pradesh, India'. *International Journal of Educational Development* 25 (3), 269–85.

VFM Unit (2004) *Statement by Value for Money Unit*. London: DfES.

Weindling, D. (1997) 'Strategic planning in schools: some practical techniques'. In M. Preedy, R. Glatter and R. Levačić (eds) *Educational Management: Strategy, Quality and Resources*. Buckingham: Open University Press.

World Bank (2002) *Achieving Education for All in Post-conflict Cambodia: Education Notes*. Washington, DC: World Bank. Available: http://www.worldbank.org/education.

World Bank (2004) *World Bank Development Report*. New York: World Bank.

Subject index

217

Author index